Gifted to:

_____

From:

_____

Date:

_____

BEYOND MEASURE.   THE POWER OF GOD GUARDS MY

ON GOD'S OFFENSIVE TEAM TODAY.   GOD IS ALWAYS

RIFY GOD.   I TAKE EVERY THOUGHT CAPTIVE.   MY

PURPOSE IS TO ENJOY GOD FOREVER.   I AM FILLED WI

SS.   I AM GOD'S BELOVED CHILD IN WHOM HE IS WEL

TIFUL BEYOND MEASURE.   THE POWER OF GOD GUARD

THE WORD OF GOD GUIDES MY STEPS.   THE FAVOR O

LEDGE HIM.   I WILL NOT LEAN ON MY OWN UNDERSTAN

52 DEVOTIONS

MORE POWER TO YOU

DECLARATIONS TO BREAK FREE
FROM FEAR &
TAKE BACK YOUR LIFE

MARGARET FEINBERG

More Power to You

© 2020 by Margaret Feinberg, LLC

Requests for information should be addressed to:
Zondervan, *3900 Sparks Dr. SE, Grand Rapids, Michigan 49546*

ISBN: 978-0-31045-556-1

Author is represented by The Christopher Ferebee Agency, www.christopherferebee.com.

Art direction: Susanna Chapman
Interior design: Emily Ghattas

Printed in China

20 21 22 23 24 25 WAI 10 9 8 7 6 5 4 3 2 1

CONTENTS

THE POWER OF DAILY DECLARATIONS

One of the benefits of forthright friends is their ability to cut through the poppycock and deliver the unvarnished truth.

A while back, my husband, Leif, and I lunched with one of our most matter-of-fact confidants, Chris. I explained how discouragement had descended without warning, stealing my joy and thrusting me into a crisis that left me ever spinning over my identity, decision-making, and future. This wasn't the type of chemically induced melancholy that could be helped by Xanax or Lexapro. I've experienced those and have zero qualms with taking medication when necessary. No, this was altogether different—more existential and more spiritual. Dark days rolled into murky months, until lostness and lethargy became my new normal.

Chris can be somewhat reserved in group settings, and he waited for me to finish my gripe session before he put down his fork, stared me straight in the eyes, and dropped a truth bomb: "I don't know how or when it happened, but you've made some agreements with the universe that just aren't true."

Startled by his bluntness, I recoiled and grew defensive, but he continued on. Over the past few years, he said, my descriptions of myself, my career, my relationships, and my perception of God had morphed. When we had first met fifteen years earlier, I cruised along with optimism and expectancy. I believed God was for me and with me, and I was capable of fulfilling my calling. I saw myself as a bridge builder, an overcomer of obstacles, a competent Bible teacher in a world where women often have to work twice as hard to gain half the opportunities of their male counterparts.

Then life happened without warning or apology. A series of brutal struggles—a cancer diagnosis, financial woes, failed friendships, a painful betrayal, unanswered prayers—all worked together to corrode my confidence, leaving me shaky and uncertain.

The confusion and discouragement left me defenseless. That's when a voice slithered in and whispered the lies . . .

You're a has-been.
You have nothing more to give.
You're a failure.
You should just give up.

I dismissed these negative ruminations at first. Then I acknowledged them and, over time, I found myself agreeing with them. Soon I was flooded by a deluge of negativity until life felt more like existing than living. Like a rudderless ship, I had grown powerless, tossed this way and that by limiting thoughts and downward spirals. I had given away the power to determine how I felt, which assumptions I lived by, how I viewed myself and others, and how I responded to conflict.

On the plane ride back from California, I searched the Scriptures for wisdom about how to change course. Right there in seat 21A, somewhere over Nevada, a verse I'd loved since childhood spoke to me as if for the first time. "Do not conform to the pattern of this world," Paul wrote in Romans 12:2, "but be transformed by the renewing of your mind." Chris was right. The negative

IF I WANTED TO TAKE BACK MY LIFE AND REGAIN MY POWER, I NEEDED TO UNTANGLE THE LIES FROM THE TRUTH.

patterns emerging in my life had arisen in my mind. I remembered that the word *repentance* (*metanoia*) literally means to change one's mind. Not just to change your behavior, but to transform your mind.

If I wanted to take back my life and regain my power, I needed to untangle the lies from the truth.

As soon as I returned home, I scoured the internet for resources on how Christians can renew their minds and stumbled on a spiritual practice used by my pastor friend, Craig Groeschel.[1] He recites particular statements of truth each day to align his thoughts with Christ's. This was just what I needed.

I snatched some paper from the printer and penned my own Daily Declarations specifically designed to confront the lies that seem to be so prevalent in my life and culture today. Starting that day, I devoted ninety seconds each morning to reading through the list—often out loud. One by one, I rejected the lies I'd accepted as truth and made bold Daily Declarations rooted in Scripture about God's goodness, the fierce love of Christ, and my worth. Seventy-two hours later, Leif said, "Something's radically different about you—you're lighter and freer than I've seen in months."

Little did I know how much this simple practice would sustain me in quarantine during the pandemic. The Daily Declarations became a spiritual lifeline that empowered me to overcome the negativity and hardship of each day.

Though it may sound hard to believe, taking ninety seconds each morning to recite these Daily Declarations has changed my life, my outlook, my impact. When the Accuser whispers in my ear, I shut him down with the truth of who God is, what God says, and who I am as God's child.

Looking back, I realize that breakdown preceded breakthrough. This is the way life so often works. When we are at our lowest, out of gas and out of options, God can work greater miracles. I now have more power in my life to pour into others, share my faith, love my spouse, overcome negative thoughts, and live out my destiny as a child of God. This is the same power that God gives to every one of his children—including you.

I bet you've made some untrue agreements with the universe too. Perhaps you've accepted the lie that your best days are behind you, that you've grown unattractive, that you're a bad parent or an inadequate spouse, that your life is less glamorous than the lives of all your "friends" on social media. These kinds of thoughts fuel our fears and insecurities.

The good news is you're here, and that tells me you're ready to expose these lies, regain control of your life, and restore the confidence you once harbored. It tells me you're willing to endure the growing pains that always accompany breakthrough. It tells me you are more powerful than you realize—because the first step to radical transformation is having the courage to show up.

I designed this devotional to empower you to experience this dynamic, effective practice of Daily Declarations in your life. You'll launch into each day with the 90-Second Challenge by reading the Daily Declarations aloud. After reciting the declarations, read through the devotions at your own pace. Each of the fifty-two entries explores the *what* and the *why* behind the declarations. These are designed to beat back the Accuser and unleash the true you.

As you embark on this life transformation, grab a journal, a pen, and a few friends. You can engage in this practice on your own, but gathering with others to reflect on your celebrations and struggles will give you more opportunities to identify what God is speaking to you, provide accountability to prevent you from stalling out, and offer you a circle of encouragers to spur you forward in your journey to embracing your best self.

If the Spirit of almighty God lives inside of you, then you are a spiritual powerhouse. God created you, called you, and equipped you. And thanks to him, there is power *for* you, *with* you, and *in* you to defeat the powers that be. The time has come for you to shake off the lies that have shackled you to shame, married you to mediocrity, and drowned you in doubt.

If you're ready to break free from shame and take your life back, then more power to you!

Margaret

THE 90-SECOND DAILY CHALLENGE

POWERFUL DAILY DECLARATIONS

Take ninety seconds each day to read the following Daily Declarations aloud. You may find one particular statement reverberating in you like a sacred echo and want to repeat that phrase a few extra times. Pay attention to what the Holy Spirit may be highlighting about you and calling you toward.

All of the Daily Declarations are deeply rooted in Scripture. For a list of the biblical references behind each one, see pages 190–193.

- Jesus is King of my life.
- I am who Christ says I am.
- I take every thought captive. I break every agreement that sets itself up against the knowledge of God.
- My purpose is to love, serve, glorify, and enjoy God forever.
- I am filled with the Holy Spirit. The same power that resurrected Christ from the dead lives in me.
- I am God's beloved child in whom he is well pleased. I am fearfully and wonderfully made, beautiful beyond measure.
- The power of God guards my thoughts, the Word of God guides my steps, and the favor of God rests on me.
- Worry is not my boss. I trust in the Lord with all my heart and lean not on my own understanding. In all my ways I will acknowledge him, and he will make my paths straight.
- The Lord is my shepherd. I lack nothing. He makes me lie down in green pastures. He leads me beside still waters. He restores my soul.
- God is my strength, my shield. He's always with me, always for me, always sees me. No weapon formed against me will prosper.
- I am anointed, empowered, and called to reach people far from God.
- My words have power. I will look for every opportunity to speak life, show compassion, and bring out the best in others.
- Shame is not my master. God's power is perfected in my vulnerability.
- I refuse to be held hostage by unforgiveness. I will forgive seventy times seven and beyond because I am forgiven.
- I am an overcomer. I refuse to bow my knee to the Accuser, listen to the voice of the Adversary, or flinch in the face of adversity.
- God works all things together for my good and his glory.
- I will look for the character and competence of God in every situation.
- I am on God's offensive team today.

1 JESUS IS KING OF MY LIFE.

LIE: I'D BE HAPPY IF ONLY _____.

"You shall have no other gods before me."
EXODUS 20:3

When Moses, the leader of the Israelites, disappears up the side of a mountain, those left behind grow restless. For all they know, their leader has fallen off a rocky ledge, never to return. The people approach Moses' brother, Aaron, and say they'll *be happy if only* they can have a god to go before them. They develop the bright idea to collect everyone's gold earrings, melt them down, and forge a gaudy cow sculpture. Then they throw a party and parade the golden bovine all over camp.

Convinced God is too difficult to follow, they create a god they can lead wherever they want.

The Lord fumes at their betrayal as Moses returns to camp with two stone tablets in hand. Moses plays interception, and God spares the lives of the Israelites. Moses becomes so incensed at their revelry, he smashes the tablets and grinds the golden calf into powder, never to be seen or celebrated again.

Moses treks up the mountain a second time. He returns with replacement tablets and hands the people carefully chiseled prohibitions on all forms of idolatry. God commands his people to neither have other gods nor make images to whom they bow a knee (Exodus 20:3–4). God doesn't mince words.

"For I, the LORD your God, am a jealous God, punishing the children for the sin of the parents to the third and fourth generation of those who hate me" (Exodus 20:5). Eek! Why does God take such a zero-tolerance policy toward other gods? God knows that it's not only the Israelites who have a penchant for crafting alternative gods who make big promises. We do too. Ours probably aren't cow shaped; instead, they may take the form of an investment account that promises protection. Or a fancy car that promises status. Or a new role that promises power. Or a house expansion that promises comfort. Or, or, or . . .

While idols may vary in form, they are all built on the same foundational assumption:

I'D BE HAPPY IF ONLY _____.

Whatever you place in that blank is also what you're placing on the throne of your life.

As author Barbara Brown Taylor observes, you can line up all these little golden calves on a mantelpiece, and almost none of them are inherently bad. The raw material of golden calves is rarely a bad thing. It's usually good. The conflict arises when a good thing is made into the ultimate thing.[1]

Like the Israelites, we're prone to reach for false gods when we're restless, when we aren't finding our satisfaction in God. That's when we eye the alternatives. Those false gods are tricky, though, because they produce results for a time. Sometimes a long time. But eventually they'll stop and turn on you with a bill that will take your breath away.

> WE WILL EXPERIENCE DIVINE RESCUE FROM DARKNESS.

God knows the damage and destruction that await when you look to anything other than him to rescue or fulfill. Your baby gods—those trinkets you give your time and attention and money to—promise to save and satisfy, but ultimately they sabotage. They make you feel good until they ensnare you with addiction. They trick you into pouring your one precious life into something that's nothing more than a bottomless pit.

The Lord has designed a better way for all of us to live. If we acknowledge Jesus as the one and only ruler of our lives, we will experience divine rescue from darkness and evil, and enter into an abundant, extravagant, eternal life. The choice is ours.

DECLARATION
JESUS IS KING OF MY LIFE.

2 I AM WHO CHRIST SAYS I AM.

LIE: I'M NOT ENOUGH.

You are a chosen people, a royal priesthood, a holy nation,
God's special possession, that you may declare the praises of
him who called you out of darkness into his wonderful light.
1 PETER 2:9

God handcrafts all of creation in abounding joy. With each day, he echoes its goodness until the sixth day, when God sculpts humanity and declares it as very good. Then a dark character slithers into the scenery and whispers a twisty truth. He suggests that God does not really want the original couple to be like God. That's why God is holding back the fruit (Genesis 3:4–5). The serpent plants seeds of inadequacy to create separation. Eve is hoodwinked into believing that if she will eat the fruit, then she will be enough.

Sometimes I wonder how Eve could have fallen for this mistruth. Yet how often I've fallen for the same falsehood. I may not say "I'm not enough" with my words, but like reaching for a forbidden fruit, my actions shout otherwise.

Looking back, I realize I started young as a pressure-cooker kid. In high school, I lived under the anxiety that I wasn't enough and worked extra hard to prove otherwise. I was so scared that I wouldn't meet expectations, apply to the right colleges, pick the right career path, win the right competitions, and earn the approval of my teachers and parents that I started bleeding inside. A doctor identified an ulcer and instructed me to dramatically decrease my stress. His advice, while necessary, added another item to my to-do list and made me feel shame for making myself sick.

Beneath the mountain of anxiety rested an insidious lie, an agreement I had made with the Accuser that I was not enough. This "not enoughness" led to a life marked by striving, discontentment, and fear.

You. Are. Not. Enough. These four words comprise one of the Enemy's cruelest and most destructive lies. Maybe you carry an unspoken feeling that you are not enough for your spouse or your children. Not enough for your parents. Not enough as a leader, teacher, coach, or employee. Not even enough for God.

This lie is so effective that in the wilderness Satan uses it on Jesus: "If you are the Son of God," then turn these stones into fresh-baked loaves, leap from the top of the temple, kneel to me and have all the kingdoms of the world. In other words, you don't have enough provision, enough power, enough potential. You. Are. Not. Enough.

Jesus counters each lie with the words "It is written . . . ," grounding himself in God's Word (Matthew 4:1–11). He allows Scripture to guide his steps and shape his responses. In the heavenly Father, Jesus is deeply loved, celebrated, and empowered. And so are you.

Later, the apostle Paul would consistently tell believers *exactly* who God said they were, and you can still use those truths to refute Satan's lie that you are not enough. Because you, yes *you*, are holy, chosen, an adopted child and heir of God. You are redeemed, forgiven, and gifted of God (Ephesians 1:1–8). You are a royal priesthood, a holy nation, and God claims you as his own (1 Peter 2:9). You're lavished with God's love—you aren't just God's friend; you're family (1 John 3:1).

YOU, YES *YOU*, ARE HOLY.

As he did with Eve in the garden and Jesus in the wilderness, the Enemy will try to convince you that you're not enough, but through the power of God's Word, you can send that viper back where he belongs. If Christ sits on the throne of your life, then he retains the final say about who you are, what you're called to do, and what you're capable of. Jesus sees you when others overlook you, he hears you when others ignore you, and he makes you more powerful than you imagine.

DECLARATION
I AM WHO
CHRIST SAYS I AM.

3 I TAKE EVERY THOUGHT CAPTIVE.

LIE: THIS IS JUST HOW IT IS.

We take captive every thought to make it obedient to Christ.
2 CORINTHIANS 10:5

My friend Holden purchased a precious puppy with whom he fell madly in love. The fluffball napped in his lap, frolicked at his feet, and won his affection in a matter of weeks. But when Holden took the dog in for a routine procedure, his beloved pet passed away on the veterinarian's table.

As I grieved with Holden, I imagined the death of my super-pup, Zoom. No dog lives forever, and I know that one day Zoom will pass on. Hearing my friend's story affected my thoughts and morphed into a fixation. I convinced myself the grim reaper was coming for my puppy just as he had snatched my friend's.

You've probably been caught in a mind spiral like this a time or two. A group of friends host a party, and you don't make the guest list. Soon you're imagining all the nasty things they were maybe, probably, definitely saying behind your back. Or a coworker outperforms you in a series of projects, and you become tormented by the idea that everyone sees you as a wash-up.

Psychologists call this "overthinking," which describes the tendency to lose control of one's thoughts and obsess over a situation with negative ruminations. Overthinking often springs from our deepest insecurities. These downward spirals can lead to anxiety, discouragement, even post-traumatic stress disorder. To numb the pain, many turn to binge-eating, binge-drinking, binge-watching, binge-anything.[1]

You ultimately become what you think.

You can choose to allow either life-giving or soul-sucking thoughts into your life. What you allow to bridle your mind will direct your day. No wonder God is so committed to drawing your attention back to him.

Neuropsychologist Donald Hebb coined the idea that the neurons that fire together wire together. That is, when we repeatedly activate neural networks or thinking patterns in our brains, these pathways thread together.[2] More simply put, you can train your brain—or, as the apostle Paul said, take every thought captive (2 Corinthians 10:5). A thought may show up to say hello, but that doesn't mean you need to rent it a room. You don't have to live under the tyranny of self-sabotaging thoughts.

YOU BECOME WHAT YOU THINK.

Pay attention to your inner dialogue. The simple act of recognizing negative thought spirals interrupts their progress. Next, redirect your mind. Replace those invalidating thoughts with Spirit-filled, life-giving ones. Whisper a prayer, a word of hope, a compliment, an exhale of gratitude. Recite a Daily Declaration, quote a scripture, sing a worship song. In doing so, you give your neural pathways the opportunity to chart a different course.

Whenever your thoughts spiral, work to identify the lie at the core of your negative thinking. Look up what Scripture says about it, denounce the lie, and declare the truth aloud with boldness. You'll be astonished at how speaking these declarations aloud strengthens you. Remember: the neurons that fire together wire together, so you *can* reroute and redeem your thinking patterns.

Find a few trusted friends to share your negative thoughts with, even if—like me—you're embarrassed to speak them. Yes, it may feel frightening at first to be so vulnerable, but you'll find that you're not alone in your struggles. The Holy Spirit will often work through your friends to reinforce the idea that these thoughts and beliefs are untrue. In the process, you'll find healing, restoration, and new freedom through the Spirit's power.

DECLARATION
I TAKE
EVERY THOUGHT CAPTIVE.

4 I BREAK EVERY AGREEMENT THAT SETS ITSELF UP AGAINST THE KNOWLEDGE OF GOD.

LIE: MY SITUATION WILL NEVER IMPROVE.

We demolish arguments and every pretension that
sets itself up against the knowledge of God.

2 CORINTHIANS 10:5

What agreements have you made with the Enemy and accepted for yourself?

After acknowledging that negative thoughts were ruling my life, I locked myself in a room with paper, pen, and prayer. There, I scribbled a list of my agreements:

> *I am ugly.*
> *I am unlovable.*
> *I am unworthy of good things or success.*
> *I'm a fraud.*
> *I should be further along by now.*
> *It's only a matter of time before the other shoe drops.*

With each new entry, hot tears streamed down my face. I had no idea how debilitating my thought life had become. I was locked in a dungeon of lies that left me alone, ashamed, afraid, trapped. Through repetition, these toxic thoughts had become lodged deep within my mind.

An *agreement* is a binding arrangement between parties as to a course of action. When you agree with something that's untrue, that agreement shapes your life until it becomes the standard by which you live.

One of the most destructive agreements you can make is that your current reality is all that will ever be. You'll never escape the dead-end job, abusive relationship, or black hole of debt. The agreement "My situation will never improve" soon becomes a self-fulfilling prophecy. You begin avoiding opportunities to escape, because you're convinced your efforts will end in failure. You become Sherlock Holmes, collecting clues that confirm the untruth that you are forever stuck right where you are.

Before you know it, your life, your potential, and your dreams wither and weaken. The agreement then becomes a stronghold that stands in the way of fulfilling your God-given destiny.

But you are not bound to this agreement and can break it whenever you choose. You have the ability to deliver a one-two power punch to any lie. The apostle Paul instructs us to "demolish arguments and every pretension that sets itself up against the knowledge of God" (2 Corinthians 10:5).

My psychologist friend, Curt Thompson, says most people who visit his office come because they have not been paying attention to what they are paying attention to. False beliefs enter our lives in childhood. They're reinforced through verbal and nonverbal cues as we age, until we develop narratives that support these false core beliefs.[1]

DELIVER A ONE-TWO POWER PUNCH TO ANY LIE.

After making my list of lies, I reviewed the entries and denounced them one by one. I named the untrue agreement and said aloud, "I break every agreement that sets itself up against the knowledge of God."

With each declaration, a sense of peace and joy saturated my spirit. Yet the process was not a one-and-done. Over the next few days, my heightened awareness revealed the many ways the same destructive agreements tried to bait me. As I became aware of a lie through the power of the Holy Spirit, I batted it down. And you can too.

If the God who made the galaxies lives inside you, then you have the power—through Christ—to denounce every destructive agreement that raises itself up against the truth of God.

Take hold of paper, pen, and prayer today. Ask God to reveal the agreements that have slipped into your life and need to be renounced. With each one, say aloud, "I break every agreement that sets itself up against the knowledge of God." Demolish them one at a time, take stray thoughts captive, and identify scriptures that counteract the lies. Then march with confidence into the freedom and abundant life God has for you.

DECLARATION
I BREAK EVERY AGREEMENT THAT SETS ITSELF UP AGAINST THE KNOWLEDGE OF GOD.

5 MY PURPOSE IS TO LOVE GOD.

We love because he first loved us.

1 JOHN 4:19

One of the quickest ways to hide a wrinkled shirt or a stain on a blouse is to add a scarf. The texture and color can make old outfits pop with new life. I started buying bargain-bin scarves in college, then splurged on more expensive ones once I landed a full-time job. Then my friend Carolyn introduced me to the cashmere scarf. *Ooh-la-la!*

Every time a fancy scarf went on sale, I scooped it up and enjoyed the temporary high of my new purchase. I loved my scarves. I'd wear a new one for the first week, then tuck it into my collection. Shopping for scarves became a pastime whenever I felt bored, frustrated, angry, or needed an escape from life's problems. Buying a scarf provided a getaway from negative feelings. Unfortunately, the escape was short-lived. My scarf-capades caught up with me one day when my loving husband asked, "Exactly how many scarves do you need?"

All of them! I wanted to respond, but held my tongue.

Realizing Leif's concern might be legitimate, I inspected my collection, which overflowed multiple drawers and filled hangers throughout my closet. That's when I discovered I owned—wait for it—113 scarves. Do you know who needs 113 scarves? No one. My stomach tightened. I had spent a mountain of cash on mindless retail therapy.

You may not have a closet full of scarves, but I bet you've felt that shopper's high before. Maybe you felt the rush from the purchase of clothing, jewelry, or a new home. Or perhaps it wasn't the item as much as the brand. You know that when people see you driving *that* make of car, carrying *that* brand of purse, sporting *that* brand of shoes, you'll have more value in their eyes.

While marketers are constantly trying to convince us that we are what we buy, the Enemy is always reinforcing the untruth that we are what we own. He wants us to be consumers above all else, enslaved to the belief that the next purchase will satisfy our deepest longings. If we just own _____, then we'll feel better, prove our worth, find our purpose, and numb any lingering pain of inadequacy. I have fallen for these lies countless times, and they always leave me tied in knots, just like my scarves.

WE WERE CREATED TO LOVE GOD—WHO DOESN'T JUST LOVE US BACK, BUT LOVED US FIRST.

Despite what advertisers suggest, our purpose is not to accumulate. If you stockpile, you'll find what you own soon owns you. Our true purpose will never be found in our purchases. None of our possessions will ever love us back. Often they make ever-increasing demands on our time, our space, our mental reserves. We end up living cluttered lives, weighed down with too much stuff instead of enjoying winsome, nimble lives.

We were created to love God—who doesn't just love us back, but loved us first. When we discover that loving God with every fiber of our being is our purpose and our mission, then we'll find our lives decluttered of everything that stands in the way of his extravagant love. We'll discover that our possessions no longer possess us because we are God's treasured possession.

Now excuse me. I need to go clean out my closet.

DECLARATION
MY PURPOSE
IS TO LOVE GOD.

6 MY PURPOSE IS TO SERVE GOD.

LIE: I NEED TO MAKE EVERYONE HAPPY.

For in him we live and move and have our being.

ACTS 17:28

For many years, I've wrestled with a degenerative condition known as *Spostas-itis*. Far too many people suffer from this syndrome in silence, and the general population is woefully uneducated about our plight. You may have been infected by the malady and not even realize it. That's because Spostas-itis can take on different forms. Maybe you recognize one of them:

> I'm *sposta* arrive early.
> I'm *sposta* stay late.
> I'm *sposta* volunteer for the extra project at work.
> I'm *sposta* bake the seventy-nine cupcakes from scratch.
> I'm *sposta* be all things to all people.

Spostas make you cranky because underneath each one is the desire to people-please, and the list of people to please never ends: employers, colleagues, teachers, coaches, friends, neighbors, parents, in-laws, spouses, children, board members, book club buddies, and on and on and on.

One of the reasons people-pleasing tempts is because it's often confused with kindness. When someone requests a favor—even when it's at great cost or inconvenience to you—you may agree to it because it's the "right thing to do" or because you don't want to appear selfish.

Hiding underneath the eagerness to please are often issues of self-worth. Saying yes to others makes you feel accepted, liked, needed. But too much people-pleasing leads to feeling overwhelmed by all you have to do, resentment toward others, and even being taken advantage of.

Some of the symptoms of Spostas-itis and people-pleasing include:

- pretending to agree with everyone
- carrying the responsibility for how other people feel
- feeling uncomfortable if someone expresses anger or disappointment toward you
- avoiding conflict at all costs
- refusing to admit when your feelings have been hurt[1]

If you experience any of these symptoms and suspect you have contracted Spostas-itis, remain calm. A cure exists. You can break the addiction to people-pleasing. Ask for the Holy Spirit's presence and wisdom. Practice saying no to a simple request, and work your way up to bigger ones. Cultivate an awareness of the kinds of people, situations, and circumstances that spark the Spostas, and be prepared to offer an alternative response next time. In the process, scout for the yeses you can dispense with joy, the ones that align with your unique gifting and God's work in your life.

You'll soon discover—quite miraculously—the world can function without you. True, some committees and organizations won't run in the exact same way. But in stepping back, you create a vacuum of opportunity for others to develop their talents. Without you as the linchpin, some events or outreaches may cease. That's okay.

BE A GOD-PLEASER, NOT A PEOPLE-PLEASER. The aim of life is to be a God-pleaser, not a people-pleaser. You're hand-crafted to love, serve, and glorify God. This is rooted in Scripture: "For in him we live and move and have our being" (Acts 17:28).

You're never "sposta" be the all-encompassing happiness factory for your entire family, office, neighborhood, church, or friend group. Stop trying to be. When you accept that the world will keep spinning without you, it will free you up to enjoy the ride.

DECLARATION
MY PURPOSE IS
TO SERVE GOD.

7 MY PURPOSE IS TO GLORIFY GOD.

LIE: MY LITTLE SIN IS NO BIG DEAL.

For all have sinned and fall short of the glory of God.
ROMANS 3:23

Sin has almost become a dirty word in our culture, but avoiding the word doesn't erase its existence. If you ever doubt the presence of sin, watch a pair of three-year-olds fight over a toy truck, spend a few hours catching up on daytime talk shows, or pause long enough in the grocery store checkout line to read a tabloid or two. Outrageous human behavior abounds.

Sin is not just "out there." It resides in all of us—you and me. The Old Testament describes sin as rebellion against God, and the New Testament adds the notion of missing the mark. Think about shooting an arrow that misses the bull's-eye and lands in the back of a friend instead. That's sin, and it puts us in league with the Enemy because that is his territory (1 John 1:8).

Sin is like rust, which forms whenever a metal containing iron is exposed to moisture and oxygen. Rust doesn't just tarnish the appearance of iron; it weakens the atomic bonds of the metal itself. Even if a steel structure looks solid on the outside, rust can cause tiny pits to form until every supporting beam becomes brittle and flaky. Given enough time and exposure to water, oxygen, and other corrosive elements, that which appears immovable will collapse.

No wonder Jesus warns against sin. He knows its corrosive nature, how it will consume us from the inside out, and if given enough time, destroy us. God fashions us to glorify him, to make much of him with our lives. And sin eats away at us until we become so far from who we're created to be that we are unrecognizable. Christ took all the world's sin upon him at the cross—that's how committed he is to seeing humanity set free from the corrosive nature of sin. Through his sacrifice, we can access forgiveness for sin when we confess and turn from it.

GOD MAKES MUCH OF HIMSELF IN YOU.

This is the last thing the Accuser wants you to do. That's why he keeps whispering so many lies regarding your sins. He tells you that your itsy-bitsy pet sin is no big deal, and you've got it under control anyway. That you can manage your sin all by yourself and you don't need to confess it, let alone seek forgiveness. That your sin isn't a sin at all—just a bad habit, and everyone has one of those.

The longer the Enemy can keep you believing his lies about sin, the deeper the corrosion will eat away at you. The remarkable good news is that through the work of Christ and his abundant grace, the corrosion can be reversed. You can be freed, scrubbed clean, made as good as new (Romans 3:23–24).

That's right! God gets us out of our messes through Christ on the cross. Repentance is the vehicle through which we confirm our dependence on Jesus. No matter what you've done or left undone, God can pluck you from the sin mess you're in and restore you. You can live your life glorifying God, meaning you can live each day making much of him. After all, God makes much of himself in you.

DECLARATION
MY PURPOSE IS
TO GLORIFY GOD.

8 MY PURPOSE IS TO ENJOY GOD FOREVER.

LIE: GOD TOLERATES ME.

Take delight in the LORD.

PSALM 37:4

Have you ever felt like you're not doing enough for God? Maybe deep inside you think you don't . . .

> pray enough
> attend church enough
> share your faith enough
> change the world enough

One of the reasons the Accuser keeps telling you you're not doing enough for God is he wants you to see God as a taskmaster and a tyrant. He wants you to believe God doesn't really love you; he merely tolerates you. Why? Because if the Accuser can convince you that you're a spiritual failure who has to earn God's approval, then he is more likely to persuade you to quit trying altogether.

Yet from the beginning God wanted only one thing from you: *you.*

The Savior has spoken love over you since time's first tick—when he fashioned you, when you took your first breath. God did not recoil when you released your first cry. He leaned in. God did not retreat in your most regrettable adolescent moment. He provided safe refuge. God did not withdraw when you raised your fist at him in anger. He opened his arms toward you. God never went silent on you, even when you went silent on him.

God cherishes you more than you cherish yourself. He adores you so much that when you were far from him, he sent his only Son, Jesus, to die for you so he could walk hand in hand with you forever (Romans 5:8). When God looks at you, he sings, dances, and shouts for joy (Zephaniah 3:17). Oh, how God enjoys you!

This is not a one-way relationship. As God delights in you, you are invited to find your delight, your greatest joy, in him. One of the most powerful ways I've discovered to increase my enjoyment of God is to linger in his presence. In other words, I don't have to end each project, each prayer, with a frantic plunge into the next item on my list. I can take time to sit in the holy silence—and so can you.

GOD WANTED ONLY ONE THING FROM YOU: *YOU.*

Lingering allows you to immerse yourself in God's affection, to experience a love so curious and powerful that it can refashion good from evil, resurrect life from death, and raise to heaven those bound for hell. In this sacred pause, you become enveloped in God's love. That's when you come to a place you've never been, but from the moment you arrive, you know you are home. This is where you belong.

Deuteronomy 4:29 whispers the promise, "You will find him if you seek him with all your heart and with all your soul."

In the lingering, your spiritual receptivity heightens. Your questions deepen. Your spirit experiences God in new ways. In the lingering, you can shift from working *for* God to being *with* God.

Sometimes when I linger, I ask God the question, "What's on your heart?" Then I pay attention to what comes to mind. Sometimes it's a conflict across the globe or a hurting friend. Other times I sense the Spirit say, "The thing that's on my heart is you."

I allow my soul and the fibers of my being to rest in his fierce love.

The next time you pray, rather than rush off to the next item on your to-do list, pause to linger. Ask God what's on his heart, and then sit in silence to hear his answer. Allow the love of God to envelop you, rest in his sacred *shalom*, and know his joy in being with you.

When the Accuser whispers that God only tolerates you, tell him to go peddle his lies elsewhere. Because you know the truth. God is madly in love with you, and you are created to enjoy him forever.

DECLARATION
MY PURPOSE IS TO ENJOY GOD FOREVER.

9 I AM FILLED WITH THE HOLY SPIRIT.

LIE: I HAVE TO DO IT ON MY OWN.

"The Advocate, the Holy Spirit, whom the Father will send in my name, will teach you all things and will remind you of everything I have said to you."

JOHN 14:26

As I've studied the Bible's many teachings about joy these past few years, I've become convinced that God has called each of us to be joy warriors. At the bedrock of this conviction is John 16:33, which says, "Be of good cheer, I have overcome the world" (NKJV).

JESUS SENT THE HOLY SPIRIT SO YOU WOULD NEVER HAVE TO GO IT ALONE.

I want to be a joy warrior, but I take little comfort in these words. I often forget Jesus has overcome the world. I think I have to survive struggles alone. Maybe you've heard the Accuser whisper, "Everything rests on your shoulders. Success and survival depend on you. Toughen up. Figure it out. Work harder. You have to do this on your own."

Jesus sent the Holy Spirit so you would never have to go it alone. When you decide to become a follower of Jesus, the Holy Spirit takes up residence in you. He makes his home in you and empowers you. Each day you are invited to yield more of your life to the Holy Spirit, who plays so many roles in your life:

When you feel overwhelmed by life, the Holy Spirit helps you.

When you're hurting and discouraged, the Holy Spirit comforts you.

When you feel lost, the Holy Spirit guides you.

When you can't find the words to pray, the Holy Spirit intercedes for you.

When you're terrified of making the wrong decision, the Holy Spirit counsels you.

When you feel fragile or shaky, the Holy Spirit strengthens you.

The Holy Spirit also brings conviction when you go awry so that you can live free from sin. He ushers in freedom (2 Corinthians 3:17), transforms you into the image of Christ (2 Corinthians 3:18), and reveals the depths of God (1 Corinthians 2:10). The Spirit is not an accessory to your life, but the one through whom all the fullness of life in Christ is experienced. The Spirit himself emanates through you. He's the source of more power to you.

The Enemy takes every opportunity to downplay the role of the Holy Spirit because he knows God's power in you makes you unstoppable.

While the Enemy is known as your Accuser or Adversary, Jesus calls the Holy Spirit your Advocate. He is with you and for you, leading and guiding, strengthening and empowering. You can lean into the Holy Spirit every day through prayer, spiritual attentiveness, and active contemplation of the Scripture.

Good cheer awaits when you remember that you are never alone. The power of the Holy Spirit resides in you, and you can turn to him for comfort, direction, strength, and wisdom. Leaning into his power shuts the mouth of the Enemy and refutes the lie that survival and success depend on you.

DECLARATION
I AM FILLED WITH THE HOLY SPIRIT.

For a free, downloadable list of the ways the Holy Spirit works in your life, visit morepowertoyoubook.com.

10 THE SAME POWER THAT RESURRECTED CHRIST FROM THE DEAD LIVES IN ME.

LIE: I'LL NEVER RECOVER FROM THIS.

And if the Spirit of him who raised Jesus from the dead is living in you . . .
ROMANS 8:11

I didn't recognize my body anymore when I looked in the mirror. The yearlong journey through chemotherapy, radiation, and multiple surgeries left my flesh battered. My body now had its first opportunity to heal, but would my raw emotions and thought life ever recover? I battled cancer; now I had to fight for a vibrant, healthy inner life again.

I didn't bounce back as I had hoped. The chemically induced brain fog clouded my mind. The chronic pain from surgeries crippled my torso. Nightmares of relapse stole my sleep. One year. Two years. Three years. Four. Somewhere along the way, the Accuser slipped in and whispered, "You'll never recover from this." I nodded in agreement.

We all encounter tragedy from which we doubt we can recover. The best friend who betrays. The child who dies from an overdose. The significant other who leaves you for someone a decade (or two) younger. Heartbreak, pain, and disappointment can make you feel as though you're clothed in rotting rags. Sometimes the road to recovery is so long, you wonder if you'll make it.

While reading the book of Mark, I stumbled on a description of some religious leaders known as the Sadducees. Convinced Jesus' journey ended in a dark tomb, they're famed for their belief that "there is no resurrection" (12:18).

How could they not believe in new life?

As I thought of how sad it is to see life this way, I sensed the Holy Spirit whisper, "You have areas in your life where you don't believe in the resurrection either." I lingered in the silence, doubting God could heal my unseen wounds, though I needed his resurrection power in those areas too.

"God, I need you every step on this road to recovery," I cried out.

I doubled down on paying attention to what I was paying attention to. I recognized all the places where I was allowing *I can't*, *It's not possible*, and *There's no way* to shape me. Each time, I asked Jesus to infuse me with his resurrection power and free me from the graveclothes of stinkin' thinkin'.

Maybe you struggle with Sadducee-thinking too. Perhaps it's easy for you to say Jesus rose from the grave, but you're still living in a tomb of past hurts, past wounds, past pains. Or perhaps you've taken up residence in the tomb of lesser living. The problem with graveclothes—beyond the stiffness and stench—is that if you wear them long enough, they become familiar, almost comfortable. Before you know it, the tomb can feel like home, until you're living like the Sadducees—with no resurrection, no hope, no new life.

THE RESURRECTION POWER LIVES IN YOU.

The resurrection power that raised Jesus from the dead lives in you. God wants to bring greater healing, wholeness, well-being to every millimeter of your life—visible and invisible. No stone is too heavy for him to roll away. No evil is too powerful for him to overcome. No sin is so stubborn that he cannot forgive. Take off your graveclothes and step into the sunlight.

DECLARATION
THE SAME POWER THAT RESURRECTED CHRIST FROM THE DEAD LIVES IN ME.

11 I AM GOD'S BELOVED CHILD IN WHOM HE IS WELL PLEASED.

LIE: I'LL NEVER BE GOOD ENOUGH.

"This is my Son, whom I love; with him I am well pleased."
MATTHEW 3:17

"You'll never amount to anything."

The teacher's words seared my ten-year-old spirit. I understood her underlying frustration. After all, I was hyperactive, easily distracted, and consumed more than my share of sugar. Oh, and I had a mega-crush on a cute boy in my class who happened to be a drummer. A drummer!

With summer nearing, all the students struggled to sit still and engage in the class project. Yet I bore the brunt of the teacher's tough day.

I don't remember any other words the teacher spoke to me that year, but I can't forget those. The harsh words stung deep inside and affirmed one of my deepest childhood insecurities. From that moment, I sealed the deal with the Accuser that I was not good enough and never would be. I lived in fear that whenever I was judged by someone else, I would always be found wanting.

The lie "I'll never be good enough" sounds a lot like "I'll never be enough" because they're ugly twins. Never-good-enough convinces you to strain and strive until you're miserable, while never-enough convinces you to quit before you even start.

We are all storytellers, and I rehearsed the narrative that if I stopped working hard—in school, at college, as a writer—then everything would disintegrate. Including me. Soon I interpreted every failure and misstep as further proof that I would never be good enough. If I scored a ninety-four on a test, I fixated on the six points I missed. If I lost eight pounds, I only saw the twenty I still had to go. Good enough always felt out of reach.

Perhaps you, too, have sensed the pangs of not being good enough. In your educational accomplishments. In your boss's eyes. In the family pecking order.

We can live our entire spiritual lives striving to hear the Master say, "Well done, good and faithful servant" (Matthew 25:23). But most days, if you're like me, you still wake up with the creeping feeling, *It's still not enough, because I'm not good enough.*

The Accuser loves this thorny lie, because it contains a half-truth. All your good works will never save you. You're right; you'll never be good enough. Only God's good work in you will be enough.

Remember, though, that it was at the beginning—not the end—of Jesus' ministry that the heavens cracked open and God's voice thundered, "This is my Son, whom I love; with him I am well pleased" (Matthew 3:17).

Each morning you can denounce the lie about your inadequacy and allow God to lavish you with his love and joy. You are *in Christ* and therefore the recipient of all his benefits, not the least of which is the fierce love and favor of the Father. Rest assured, the stunning good work God is doing in you, he will bring to completion. What if you took up residence in this confidence and security? How would that change the landscape of your life?

YOU ARE *IN CHRIST.*

Today is the day to break free from the unrealistic standards you've been striving to achieve. Declare the words "I am God's beloved child in whom he is well pleased." Look for opportunities to slip these words into conversations about others and watch their eyes widen in disbelief. As you live into this truth, you'll find the silly measuring sticks of enough-ness shortening, then vanishing. The score, the rating, matters less when God's unmerited favor matters more.

DECLARATION
I AM GOD'S BELOVED CHILD IN WHOM HE IS WELL PLEASED.

12 I AM FEARFULLY AND WONDERFULLY MADE.

I praise you because I am fearfully and wonderfully made;
your works are wonderful, I know that full well.
PSALM 139:14

I was put on my first diet when I was nine years old. Always the "round one," I felt comfortable in my skin until a classmate commented about my large backside. I don't know how enormous a rear end can really be when you're in fifth grade, but I remember my classmate's words inflicting so much shame.

After that, I loathed my body. To ensure no one ever stood behind me, I tucked myself toward the back of every line. I was always hungry and tried not to eat too much. At the table, I felt as if I never received enough nourishment.

Those childhood wounds seeped into adulthood. Sometimes I still find myself calculating calories and reviewing the day's consumption to determine whether I overate.

Did I eat too many carbs? Too little protein? Not enough vegetables?

A tasty culinary experience with loved ones can become an opportunity to judge myself harshly. Over the years, I've heard from so many others who recount similar stories of shame. Maybe you, too, have felt shame about your appetite, relationship with food, or body.

We live in a world with countless fad diets, and we're bombarded with photoshopped images. When we look in the mirror, we may feel shame or turn away in disgust—that is, if we can muster the courage to look in the mirror at all.

The Accuser pounces, often using comparison, to reinforce negative beliefs (*You're not thin enough, not shapely enough*) or that you're too much (*You have too many pounds, too many wrinkles*). The Enemy heaps a double serving of shame on your physical appearance in hopes that

YOU ARE FEARFULLY AND WONDERFULLY MADE.

you'll soon feel the same way about your soul. All too often we nod in agreement with these statements, until we find ourselves labeling parts of our body as misshapen, or worse, repulsive.

Yet we are not to be ashamed. We are precious creations fashioned in the image of God. We are objects of our Creator's love.

Yes, you. *You* are fearfully and wonderfully made. *You* are embedded with wonder upon wonder. The essence of true beauty is the glory of Christ in *you*. Our infinite God created you to display a facet of his glory in this world. To view yourself as anything less shouts an insult to the Artist who fashioned you.

The key to breaking free from the Accuser's lies is tucked into today's verse. Begin by praising God for the way he made you. All of you. Every physical inch of you. Praise him each day until you know "full well" how God sees you. As a child of God, you are beautiful beyond measure and a one-of-a-kind masterpiece.

DECLARATION
I AM FEARFULLY AND WONDERFULLY MADE.

13 I AM BEAUTIFUL BEYOND MEASURE.

LIE: GETTING OLDER IS THE WORST.

You are altogether beautiful.
SONG OF SONGS 4:7

Walking through Costco, I spotted a makeup mirror on sale and scooped it into my basket. But let me tell you a little something: this wasn't an average mirror—it was a whopping, twenty-times-magnification mirror with a fancy fluorescent light. I rushed home, plugged in my new toy, flipped on the light, leaned close, and gasped at what I saw.

Every pore became a crater, every scar a deep indent, every blotch a dark stain. This magnification mirror made me look twenty times worse, twenty times older, and twenty times more likely to return my purchase. (Luckily, Costco has the world's most gracious return policy.)

The aging process presents new challenges for all of us. Our metabolisms screech to a halt without warning. Crow's feet march across our faces in a blink. Age spots arise out of nowhere. Body parts droop, sag, then drag. In a culture that glorifies youth, these changes can make us feel as if we're losing our worth. Yet as followers of Jesus, we are radiant at every age because the Lord's presence is in us.

Moses experienced wondrous encounters with the Divine, from the burning bush to the Egyptian plagues. One of my favorites occurs when Moses climbs Mount Sinai and receives the Ten Commandments. He returns radiant. Everyone can see the divine glow, the favor and authority of God, on Moses (Exodus 34:29).

AS FOLLOWERS OF JESUS, WE ARE RADIANT.

The radiance fades with time. Moses has to encounter God again and again for another recharge of divine glory. The apostle Paul writes that this powerful leader veiled his face to prevent the Israelites from seeing the fading away (2 Corinthians 3:13).

Yet we are not like Moses.

You can scrap the veil because the radiance that fills you as a child of God does not fade. You are in Christ—the Light of the World—and the splendor of God resides in you.

If God held a magnifying mirror up to you, he would see Christ glorified in you. Unlike earthly mirrors that highlight imperfections, Christ in you is ever expanding and intensifying.

Paul continues: "And we all, who with unveiled faces contemplate the Lord's glory, are being transformed into his image with ever-increasing glory, which comes from the Lord, who is the Spirit" (2 Corinthians 3:18).

The presence of Christ makes you glow in every age and stage. The life of Christ makes you luminous. The light of Christ makes you radiant. This is who you are each day. No amount of wrinkles can change that. You are beautiful beyond measure.

DECLARATION
I AM BEAUTIFUL
BEYOND MEASURE.

14 THE POWER OF GOD GUARDS MY THOUGHTS.

LIE: THE WORLD IS TOTALLY MESSED UP.

Whatever is true, whatever is noble, whatever is right, whatever is pure, whatever is lovely, whatever is admirable—if anything is excellent or praiseworthy—think about such things.
PHILIPPIANS 4:8

Some days the darkness overwhelms me:

> A toddler with stage 4 cancer.
> A hardworking friend laid off from Covid-19.
> A faithful gal who has another miscarriage.
> A loving father with early-onset dementia.

I lift their names in prayer, but my heart still sinks. *How long, Lord?*

A quick scan of headlines worsens my resolve. Oppression stifles the globe. Abandoned children with no refuge. Innocents swept away as collateral damage in an unjust war. Another mass shooting. Bodies stacked in the street from the pandemic. A cauldron rather than a melting pot of a nation.

In the age of social media and 24/7 news, the darkness feels impossible to avoid and emotionally draining. If we listen to the doom-and-gloom narrative long enough, despair sets up shop in us. We ache for a word of encouragement, a prayer to offer, a spiritual breakthrough—any shaft of light to break up the blackness and restore hope.

THE SECRET TO SURVIVING WHAT'S HAPPENING *AROUND* YOU IS DISCOVERING GOD'S POWER *IN* YOU.

The apostle Paul was accustomed to darkness too. Beset by endless hardships—imprisonment, malnourishment, shipwrecks, ridicule—Paul managed to hold fast to God's goodness. In his letter to the Philippian church, he shares the formula for cultivating defiant hope in the midst of darkness:

> Finally, brothers and sisters, whatever is true, whatever is noble, whatever is right, whatever is pure, whatever is lovely, whatever is admirable—if anything is excellent or praiseworthy—think about such things. (Philippians 4:8)

The secret to surviving what's happening *around* you is discovering God's power *in* you. You don't have to become ensnared in the speculation and scandals, the darkness and dread, the horror and hostilities.

The world is never totally messed up, because God remains in control. Above all the chaos, a God of order reigns. Just because circumstances are bad doesn't mean God isn't up to something good.

Paul equips you to defeat the Accuser's voice. This passage-turned-prayer empowers you to live with hope. Pray right now:

Jesus, draw my awareness to . . .

Whatever is true: Open my eyes to the stunning truth founded in Christ and displayed as rock solid as granite.

Whatever is noble: Open my heart to see your rule and reign, your character and competence, in this world.

Whatever is right: Open my mind to recognize the fullness of your loving justice and unending grace.

Whatever is pure: Open my will to stand in holy awe of you and submit to your refining in my life.

Whatever is lovely: Open my ears to be attuned to your words, actions, and presence in me, around me, through me.

Whatever is admirable: Open my mouth to speak in ways that demonstrate respect for others. Help me infuse others with courage today. Amen.

Supernatural power safeguards your thoughts whenever you direct them Christward. God is working in powerful, redemptive ways, and he's dropping breadcrumbs of goodness all over the place. It's your job to notice and spread them everywhere you go. As you do, you'll rise up as a blazing beacon of hope in an anxious, panicky world.

DECLARATION
THE POWER OF GOD GUARDS MY THOUGHTS.

15 THE WORD OF GOD GUIDES MY STEPS.

LIE: I HAVE NO IDEA WHAT TO DO NEXT.

Thy word is a lamp unto my feet, and a light unto my path.
PSALM 119:105 KJV

When Leif and I were first married, he worked at the airport for TSA, which we joked stood for "Take Your Stuff Away." He rose in the ranks until he managed all the airports in southeast Alaska. The job—and the incriminating acts of others—took a heavy toll on him. Leif launched an investigation and, in return, received retribution. The work environment grew so hostile he was forced to quit. Leif applied for other government jobs, but each required a recommendation from his former boss. Every door he attempted to open was bolted shut.

"I have no idea what to do next," he confessed.

Sitting beside Leif, I nestled into the crook of his neck. Over the last six months, I'd watched him deteriorate. He had lost countless nights of sleep and gained weight. His hair thinned and sprouted gray; his eyesight weakened. How do you find a way forward when there's no way forward?

"We may not know what is next," I whispered. "But we do know what to do next. Let's pray."

Together, we confessed our sense of injustice, our fear, our frustrations. We handed God the heaviest weights—the loss of income and insurance, the loss of profession and direction, the loss of the life we once had. We did not tell God anything he did not already know. When we exhaled our "amen," we both reached for our Bibles. Leif turned to his most beloved book, Philippians, and read, "Let your gentleness be evident to all. The Lord is near" (4:5).

I flipped to Isaiah and read mine, "Do not fear, for I have redeemed you; I have summoned you by name; you are mine. When you pass through the waters, I will be with you; and when you pass through the rivers, they will not sweep over you. When you walk through the fire, you will not be burned; the flames will not set you ablaze" (43:1–2).

Over the next few months, we didn't just cling to these passages; we white-knuckled them. We clutched them tight as we packed everything we owned onto a ferry. As we landed jobless in Seattle. As we drove to my home state of Colorado. As we lived in a borrowed apartment, searching for an affordable place to live.

Somewhere along the way, amid prayer and Scripture, the thought emerged, *What if we teamed up on my writing and speaking?* We jumped at the idea with only enough funds to survive for sixty days. So we clung to the Scriptures every single day. At the end of two months, we had earned enough for sixty more days. God continued to provide for us for the next eight years, until Leif started working at a church— another giant leap of faith.

WITH CHRIST YOU ALWAYS KNOW WHAT TO DO NEXT.

In times when God repositions you in his kingdom, the Enemy likes to paralyze you with the belief, "I have no idea what to do next." As a child of God, you already know exactly what to do: seek God in prayer and press your nose deep into Scripture.

You may not know what is next, but with Christ you always know what to do next. God's Word will lead you, guide you, sustain you. Other people will speak words that encourage you, but God's Word will speak words that empower you for the next great adventure he has for you.

DECLARATION
THE WORD OF GOD GUIDES MY STEPS.

16 THE FAVOR OF GOD RESTS ON ME.

LIE: IT MUST BE MY FAULT.

Grace and peace to you from God our Father and the Lord Jesus Christ.
PHILIPPIANS 1:2

I once worked with an editor who had a habit of sending ambiguous emails that sent me into tailspins. He said things like:

We need to jump on a call right now.
This is so important—let's connect ASAP.
You need to know something. Reach out quick.

My chest always cinched. Did I miss a deadline? Fail to deliver something I promised? Post something terrible on social media and not realize it? What if my publisher is done with me f-o-r-e-v-e-r? I'll never be able to write again. It's over, over, over.

Once, when I called my editor back, he shared with excitement that he and his wife were adopting a child from Uganda. I was thrilled to be among the first to know, but how much mental energy and anguish had I wasted in the meantime?

My response revealed I had adopted one of the Enemy's agreements as my default response: "It must be my fault." You may have fallen

"GRACE AND PEACE" PROVIDES MORE THAN A TAGLINE.

for this one too. When you receive an ambiguous message, your mind darts to the insistent thought: *Tragedy is impending, and it's likely my fault.* You have no evidence for making such a conclusion, but it still sends you spinning.

I've since found comfort in the words of the apostle Paul: "Grace and peace to you from God our Father and the Lord Jesus Christ" (Philippians 1:2). He begins his correspondence with a three-word blessing that's more than pleasantry, formality, or cliché: "Grace and peace."

If you scan the New Testament, you'll discover "Grace and peace" is Paul's standard salutation. The phrase and concept proved so critical for the apostle that every one of his New Testament letters opens with this greeting. Most end with it too.

Grace is God's favor, and it describes God's character and actions toward his people. This gift of God cannot be earned or deserved. Some have dubbed it "the Gospel in a word."[1]

You may be tempted to think God's favor is for others, those who live far holier lives. Yet the Bible reveals God's favor on David, who committed adultery; Rahab, who lived sultry; Abraham, who lied; Peter, who denied; and Jacob, who vied. The evidence is stacked high. No one is worthy of God's favor. Yet God bestows this gracious gift on his children—including you.

Paul couples favor with *peace*, a word that alludes to more than well-being; it's a satisfaction, fulfillment, and wholeness. This kind of peace isn't based in the absence of something—stress, trials, or hardship—but the presence of Someone. This peace manifests as deep, transforming, holistic shalom with God, with others, and within. "Grace and peace" provides more than a tagline; it's a blessing, a benediction, an invitation, and a promise.

Sooner or later you'll face an impossible situation. The odds will be stacked against you. The Accuser will sneak into the room and tempt you to assume fault when you have done nothing wrong. Instead of believing this lie, offer a fierce holy rebuttal: "Grace and peace."

DECLARATION
THE FAVOR OF GOD
RESTS ON ME.

17 WORRY IS NOT MY BOSS.

"Therefore I tell you, do not worry about your life."
MATTHEW 6:25

If you've ever experienced a bout of panic or been diagnosed with an anxiety disorder, you're not alone. The US leads the world in anxiety, and tens of millions of us are dependent on prescription anxiety medications to make it through the day.[1] Worry isn't a modern-day invention. When the word *worry* first appeared in English, it meant "to strangle." Over the centuries, *worry* transitioned to mean "to bite and shake," much like a dog with a rubber toy. Then the understanding of the word shifted to "harass or vex." In the early nineteenth century, *worry* adopted the more modern meaning "to make or be persistently anxious."[2]

The development of this word reveals that a touch of worry can inflict a heap of harm. Like me, you probably experienced epic waves of worry during the pandemic. It can paralyze you in fear, steal your dreams, and cause you to lash out at those you love. I am most at risk of having a blow-up with my husband when I am trapped in a cycle of worry.

Take a single problem, add worry, and watch it multiply like baby bunnies. The modern world dispenses endless reasons for concern, so if you're worry-prone, the Accuser has ample opportunities to convince you that you can't break free. Soon worry becomes your boss and runs the show. Rather than make tomorrow better, it drains you of your strength and disempowers you.

This rings true in our bodies, emotions, and brains. A Princeton University study found that people preoccupied with financial worry see a drop in cognitive function equal to losing an entire night's sleep or the equivalent of thirteen IQ points.[3] The hormones released during episodes of stress are known to contribute to memory loss and cause brain damage—which is enough to make you worry about what you're already worrying about.

Jesus tells us time and time again not to worry and teaches that worry always takes, never gives. It won't even add a single hour to your life—and in fact, it may steal several (Matthew 6:27).

How do you break free from the cycle of overwhelming anxiety?

The apostle Paul says prayer can alleviate many of our worries: "Do not be anxious about anything, but in every situation, by prayer and petition, with thanksgiving, present your requests to God" (Philippians 4:6).

When believers pray, great things happen. For starters, every prayer is itself a miracle. You are communicating with the living God, the Creator of all. Remarkably, no prayer you offer is too insignificant, no request too immense. God cares for all the concerns of all his children.

Second, prayer opens you up to be used by God for the work of his kingdom as you gain a throne-room perspective. You get new eyes, unclouded by worry and sharpened toward a true vision of God and his kingdom.

WHEN BELIEVERS PRAY, GREAT THINGS HAPPEN. Prayer also offers a great privilege. Through prayer you can hand God all your needs, all your concerns, all that triggers your anxiety. You don't need to hold back. Paul suggests giving God your fears coupled with gratitude, because thanksgiving provides a powerful antidote to anxiety.

What will you receive in return for your anxious prayers? The exact opposite of worry: peace. Not just any ordinary kind of peace, but a deep shalom—the peace that contrasts with the life-stealing nature of worry. More than a lack of conflict, the shalom peace conveys the blessing that overflows when one lives in right relationship with God. The peace of God acts as a guardrail against the downward spiral of fear and fuels your life as an overcomer.

You will never get rid of all the what-ifs and what-if-nots in your life, but when they come, you can rest assured that you do not meet them alone. God remains with you. Lift up your prayers; offer up your gratitude; receive God's settling shalom.

DECLARATION
WORRY IS NOT MY BOSS.

18 I TRUST IN THE LORD WITH ALL MY HEART.

LIE: I NEED TO BE IN CONTROL.

Trust in the LORD with all your heart.

PROVERBS 3:5

One thing I dislike most about myself is my tendency to be a complete control freak.

If you come to my house for a dinner party, you'll see me rush around, filling people's glasses—even if they say they don't want a refill. I'll interrupt friends mid-sentence to tell them they're talking too loud. I won't just tell you there's tomato sauce on your chin; I'll wipe it off myself as if I'm your mother. I'll even sometimes catch myself telling people how to manage their careers, relationships, or finances when they never asked for my advice. These acts can seem innocuous on their own, but each behavior reinforces the false and harmful agreement, "I need to be in control at all times." A sense of control entices because it provides the illusion of certainty in an unpredictable world.

Our efforts to control are often just attempts to reduce life to a series of if-thens. *If* we control the situation, *then* we're guaranteed a desired outcome. This works stupendously . . . until it doesn't. A difficult diagnosis, the loss of a loved one, a tragic accident. Hard, horrible things we could never predict happen in this world, and we're left reeling in our finite humanness.

Life isn't a mere machine we can manipulate, which is why control freakery guarantees a shortcut to Disappointmentville. No matter how much we assume we are in control, it's only a matter of time until we're reminded that we're not.

My controlling nature is the carefully laid sod over my buried secret that elsewhere in my life I feel so out of control. Maybe you have places where you feel this way too. You, too, may be tempted to regain a sense of control through unhealthy habits:

- Do you micromanage others?
- Are you regularly trying to "help" people change?
- Do you grapple with not being in the know?
- Is your daily life shaped by what you imagine other people think or see when they look at you and your family?

These types of behaviors come with hefty price tags. Attempting to manage every contingency plan in every situation is exhausting. It will make you and everyone around you miserable. And if you control others too much, it's only a matter of time before they pull away. This includes your parents and children, spouse and friends. In addition, trying to control what other people think about you and your family will wear you out. It's frustrating, because controlling everything is a game you'll never win.

Whenever you try to control what you cannot, you lose control of the one thing that you can: yourself.

The Bible uses an antiquated word to describe the real issue with control freakery: *idolatry.* This is what the Scripture labels any effort to trust something or someone other than God to save, satisfy, or rule the future. Every time I reach for the joystick of control, I am telling God that he's not good at his job.

CEDE MANAGEMENT OF YOUR LIFE TO THE ONE WHO CONTROLS ALL THINGS.

If you're rushing about, trying to control your life—and maybe the lives of those around you— then I want to challenge you. You don't have to live this way. Each day you can wake up, take a breath, and cede management of your life to the One who controls all things. When you're tempted to take back the reins of life, boldly declare, "I trust in the Lord with all my heart."

Here. Let me refill your drink as you learn to let go.

DECLARATION
I TRUST IN THE LORD
WITH ALL MY HEART.

19 I WILL NOT LEAN ON MY OWN UNDERSTANDING.

Do not lean on your own understanding.
PROVERBS 3:5 NASB

Several years ago, my counselor challenged me to read the book *Boundaries* by Henry Cloud and John Townsend.

"I've read it maybe five or six times," I replied.

"That's amazing," he said, "because you haven't put a single thing from the book into practice!"

I burst out laughing because I knew my counselor was right. When I was younger, I believed success required me to keep serving, keep sacrificing, keep going until I had nothing left to give. I tried to be everything to everyone. If I collapsed into bed exhausted, I believed the day was well spent. I was leaning on my own understanding and yielding withered fruit.

It's taken me years—and rereading *Boundaries* a few more times—to realize that Jesus is the only one capable of being the Messiah.

We can easily believe the lie that we, too, must be saviors. We pick up the cloth of hard work and begin sewing our initiatives, in our strength, with our intentions. Our motivation isn't always bad. We want to make a difference.

If we're honest, though, sometimes our refusal to say no comes from far unhealthier places. We want the satisfaction of "fixing" something or someone. We want to be heroic. Or we want to avoid conflict. *Ouch.*

Perhaps your conflict aversion emerges from previous ugly fights, fear of consequences, or undervaluing yourself. Whatever the cause, you may be driven to say yes to your colleague, supervisor, or best friend because you don't want to experience fallout. Perhaps this even happens with your children. Secretly, you fear if you say no too many times, they'll stop loving you.

JESUS IS THE ONLY ONE CAPABLE OF BEING THE MESSIAH.

Our lack of boundaries and inability to say no comes at a high cost. Often in the process of trying to save the world with all our yeses, we end up disregarding what God wants to do in and through us. We turn the company around, but we neglect the kids. We support the grieving friend, but we ignore the spouse's emotional needs. We volunteer in our community, but we become inattentive to aging parents. Whenever we believe we cannot say no, we forget that we are not the Messiah, we cannot solve every problem, and we cannot meet every need.

> Do you push yourself too hard or too far?
> Do you expect too much from yourself?
> Do you wrestle with perfectionism?

The actual Messiah appears as the only one among us *without* a Messiah complex. He doesn't strive or strain. At times, Jesus withdraws to more deeply align himself with the Father.

Jesus reveals, "Very truly I tell you, the Son can do nothing by himself; he can do only what he sees his Father doing, because whatever the Father does the Son also does" (John 5:19).

The Savior invites you into this same kind of alignment with him and with the Father. You can retreat to take time to pray, reflect, and ask for wisdom. You can slow your roll with the yeses. If someone demands an immediate response, you can let them know you're not comfortable with that. Gently let the person know that if they need someone who can offer a fast response, that's not you.

Because of Christ, you don't have to stress to save the world. He's already done it for you.

DECLARATION
I WILL NOT LEAN ON
MY OWN UNDERSTANDING.

20 IN ALL MY WAYS
I WILL ACKNOWLEDGE HIM.

LIE: I'M TOO BUSY FOR THAT.

In all your ways acknowledge Him.

PROVERBS 3:6 NASB

I arrived in Utah ready to say yes to every new adventure and fresh face. Invitations to hike and ski and wander the farmers market flooded my in-box. I jumped at the opportunity to grab a latte with a new friend and explore a trail or town event.

A mere thirty-six months later, however, the tenor of my life changed. Feeling more settled into our new life, I said nah to anything that didn't align with my already packed schedule. I revisited familiar trails in my free time, skied only the best weather days, and traded the farmers market for the grocery store on the nearest corner. I grew less responsive, less flexible, less open to new adventures.

This seeped into my spiritual life too. Reading Scripture became a rote act confined to a well-defined time period. I prayed the same tired prayers. The rings of my life contracted as I engaged in only that which was easy, familiar, and comfortable. I even started to ignore divine nudges to "Go back and apologize" or "Encourage this person today." I was too busy for that. Or so I told myself.

I'd fallen into a rut and become a naysayer to any new leadings of the Spirit. Then one day I stumbled on the story of a similarly sour person in John's gospel. Jesus calls Philip to become a disciple. Philip barrels toward his friend Nathanael to deliver the remarkable news that they've found the Messiah (John 1:45).

Nathanael appears unfazed. He asks if anything good can possibly come from Nazareth (John 1:46). Philip delivers an incredible gift—an invitation to meet the long-awaited Messiah—and Nathanael responds with a hearty "nope."

Philip persists with a new, three-word invitation: "Come and see."

That's when Nathanael transforms from a naysayer to a yaysayer. After encountering Jesus, Nathanael says, "Rabbi, you are the Son of God" (John 1:49).

It's easy to use naysaying to live a more comfortable life, where everything feels safe and controlled. Anyone can swing the pendulum toward spiritual laziness, where you do less and less, forgetting that God wants to use you in his big, bold redemption plan.

As God's child, you're called to trade in naysaying for yaysaying. You're called to wake up each day and "in all your ways acknowledge Him" (Proverbs 3:6 NASB). You're created to live wide-eyed for the ways God wants to meet you and use you.

I have added a one-question prayer into my morning routine: "Holy Spirit, what do you want me to do today?" Then I sit, wait, listen, discern, and jot down anything that comes to mind. The list includes simple activities: a reminder to reconnect with a friend, a message to encourage my readers, or an admonition to listen more than I speak. With rare exception, the Holy Spirit leads me outward toward others-oriented practices. None of the calls to act seem burdensome. They feel, well, *joyful.*

YOU'RE CALLED TO TRADE IN NAYSAYING FOR YAYSAYING.

Go ahead. Be bold. Cry out to God, "Holy Spirit, what do you want me to do today?"

Say yes to new opportunities, relationships, and fresh ways of connecting with God's Word. Each and every day when you wake up, you are invited to leap out of bed to "Come and see!" as if Christ has just moved to town and wants to lead you on a grand adventure.

DECLARATION
IN ALL MY WAYS
I WILL ACKNOWLEDGE HIM.

21 HE WILL MAKE MY PATHS STRAIGHT.

LIE: I SHOULD BE FURTHER ALONG BY NOW.

He will make your paths straight.

PROVERBS 3:6 NASB

Mother's Day doesn't always show up with a vase of lilies and breakfast in bed. For many, the holiday delivers a hybrid of pride and pain, joy and cynicism, hope and heartbreak.

Perhaps you lost your momma or never knew her. Or your relationship became strained. Maybe you pray for the positive pregnancy test, or you've sojourned through a failed adoption. Maybe you avoid baby showers because you know someone will ask, "So when are you having kids?"

In the Bible, a woman named Hannah shares the ache of childlessness. She prays fervently for a baby and hears nothing, nada, zilch-a-mundo. The Accuser's taunts are never disclosed, but we can imagine the barbs: "This should have already happened. You're not getting any younger, you know. Tick tock, tick tock."

As the curtain peels back on Hannah's story, a tangled marital web of jealousy, rivalry, and favoritism emerges. Even worship fails to provide a safe haven for Hannah. The sight of another woman with children accentuates the pain. Year after year, the Accuser pricks her with the lie that she should be further along.

The Accuser always attacks God's timeline. Why? If he can convince you that God is delayed or a no-show, then you'll be tempted to doubt his power and love. Like Eve in the garden, you'll be tempted to take matters into your own hands. That's why the Enemy screams that your start-up, your marriage, your kiddos, your retirement plan, your relationship with God should be further along by now.

GOD WORKS ALL THINGS FOR GOOD—YES, EVEN THIS.

Even when Hannah believes her hope has dried up, that she has nothing left to offer except salty tears and a withering womb, she worships God through sacrifice and prayers.

In God's infinite goodness, Hannah's prayers don't go unheeded. Hannah trusts in the God of Abraham—a God who heard the cries of Sarah and provided a son. Hannah trusts in the God of Moses—a God who heard the cries of his people in slavery and rescued them.

In her prayers, she tosses out an anchor of hope, promising her future son to the Lord's service. Hannah believes so fervently in God's *ability* to hear her cries and open her womb, she even makes a promise that hinges on God's response. Eventually, Hannah gives birth to a baby boy, affirming that God hears silent prayers.

You may never receive the answers you desire, but your cries echo in God's presence. In his infinite wisdom, God works all things for good—yes, even this. Whatever you're facing, you can ask God to infuse you with courage to speak the unutterable desires of your heart and know that your requests have not fallen on deaf ears.

Consider making an Abundance Journal to refocus your thoughts and attention. Each day write down the extra graces, surprise gifts, and gentle kindnesses you receive. Write down the miracles God is working in and through you. What are you able to experience now that you couldn't if you received what you wanted? How are you becoming more like Christ even in this?

You are not falling behind. God has you right where you are supposed to be, no matter what day of the year it is.

DECLARATION
HE WILL MAKE
MY PATHS STRAIGHT.

22 THE LORD IS MY SHEPHERD.

LIE: I'M JUST NOT THAT SMART.

The Lord is my shepherd.

PSALM 23:1

Throughout Scripture, Jesus highlights natural wonders to explain supernatural truths. From fruitless fig trees and buzzing bees to choking weeds and lost sheep, the Bible is steeped in an agrarian culture.

I never used to think about sheep much. Or shepherds, for that matter. Then I traveled to visit my new friend, Lynn, and spent time with her flock. We traversed muddy trails, wandered through grassy fields, and spent long days nestled among her two dozen sheep. Without even trying, I fell in love with these woolly creatures.[1]

One of the great mistruths taught in churches today is that sheep are dumb. Studies reveal sheep possess elaborate cognitive abilities as well as recognition skills comparable with humans. Sheep can identify their shepherd's face from dozens of other photographs. They can be trained much like dogs by using clickers and reward systems. One YouTube video shows them navigating difficult obstacle courses, *American Ninja Warrior*–style.

The teaching that sheep are unintelligent has done immense harm to our understanding of God and how he sees us. The Bible often refers to God's people as sheep. Accept the myth of sheep imbecility, and it's easy to see yourself as an unintelligent creature who needs God for the sole purpose of overcoming stupidity. If you believe sheep are dumb, then you'll read the seven hundred references to sheep and flocks throughout Scripture as if God is saying, "You are dumb. You are dumb. You are dumb."

Sheep's strange behavior, which includes walking off cliffs if left unattended, is sometimes seen as evidence of low intelligence. As I discovered, the issue is much more complex. Sheep are not dumb; they are defenseless. Unlike other animals, they lack razor teeth. They don't even make scary, aggressive noises. When was the last time *ba-a-a-ah* scared anyone? The only defense mechanism God provides sheep is living within a flock under the watchful eye of a good shepherd.

If a shepherd deserts the flock, and a sheep becomes distracted and wanders off, all the rest will follow. Why? Because their only safety mechanism is to stay close together. Without a good shepherd, it's only a matter of time before they overeat, consume poisonous vegetation, become prey, or wander into dangerous territory—all due to their God-given protection strategy: groupthink.

The earliest Christians clung to the symbol of Jesus as Good Shepherd. First-century Jesus followers felt defenseless against Rome's might. They were as likely to use a shepherding symbol for Christ as we are to use crosses today.

Maybe you've thought, *I'm just not that smart.* What a terrible representation of who you are and who God has made you to be. You are more powerful than you think! You are not dumb.

God created you defenseless so that you will trust him as your defender. The psalmist uses vivid metaphors for God and his protective nature: a rock, refuge, shield, and stronghold. God wants us to turn to him for protection, provision, and guidance in all things as our Good Shepherd (Psalm 23:1). Even the mighty warrior David identified himself as a sheep when penning his popular psalm.

YOU ARE MORE POWERFUL THAN YOU THINK!

The next time you hear someone say, "Sheep are dumb," gently correct them: "No, sheep are not dumb; they are defenseless and created to depend on God as their Defender."

In what area of your life have you been trying to defend yourself instead of turning to God to defend you? Today the Good Shepherd invites you to come to him. He wants to scoop you up in his arms, where you are safe and secure.

DECLARATION
THE LORD IS MY SHEPHERD.

23 I LACK NOTHING.

I lack nothing.

PSALM 23:1

I adore looking through online photos of friends and seeing their everyday lives. But sometimes when I'm scrolling, a subtle lie creeps in: "They have it so much better than me." Their lives appear perfect; their kitchens appear cleaner; even their dogs pose on command, while mine obeys only when he feels like it.

When was the last time you opened social media and felt a pinch of envy? Or you saw a well-dressed woman with a dream body and dream spouse and dream children and felt jealousy well up inside you? Or you drove by the gates of that fancy neighborhood and thought, *Must be nice to live there?*

The comparison trap abounds in the digital age. We fall into its vices whenever we focus on how we measure up to someone else. It's easy to forget everyone is fighting battles—especially when they're so skillfully hidden.

How often have you posted an image or video on social media that made your life appear better than it is? Or if a friend asks how you are, have you ever cherry-picked details to minimize the difficulties you're experiencing? We all do this. Even the most famous people in the Bible weren't immune to comparisons and the desire to come out on top.

Moses is revered by Christians and Jews as a portrait of poise and leadership. He stood up to a powerful ruler, served up mind-bending miracles, and freed up a nation from slavery.

As a young man, Moses appears as a mere desert nomad tending a flock in the wilderness. Then one night Moses discovers a bush ablaze with the voice of God flaming inside. The Almighty informs Moses

EVERYONE IS FIGHTING BATTLES.

that he's getting a job promotion—from the shepherd of a flock to the spokesperson of a nation. It's a good gig, and you can't beat the benefits package. But Moses isn't sure he's qualified because of his slow speech and lack of eloquence (Exodus 4:10).

I've always been puzzled by Moses' insecurity. The leader delivers a litany of powerful speeches in subsequent chapters. Even the first Christian martyr, Stephen, describes Moses as "powerful in speech and action" (Acts 7:22). How do you suppose Moses came to believe such a lie?

The text tells us Moses started making this agreement in the past. I imagine Moses as an adopted orphan in Pharaoh's house surrounded by educated and well-spoken royals. Skilled orators flock to the court and deliver powerful speeches intended to persuade and impress. From the periphery, Moses must think, *They have it so much better than me. I could never do that. I am slow of speech and tongue.* Just like that, the legendary leader probably tumbled into the comparison trap.

Years later, under a canopy of stars, God shatters the Accuser's agreement that has enslaved Moses: "Who gave human beings their mouths? . . . Is it not I, the LORD? Now go; I will help you speak and will teach you what to say" (Exodus 4:11–12).

God reminds Moses that he's not walking this spinning rock alone. The Great Giver of good gifts sojourns with him and provides everything necessary to carry out his calling.

You may not have the most photogenic family, an immaculate kitchen, or a perfectly trained dog, but you can still find peace and contentment in the richness of your relationship with God. You can lean into the promise of Philippians 4:19: "God will meet all your needs according to the riches of his glory in Christ Jesus."

Regardless of where you find yourself each minute, hour, day, month, or year, you can live in the reality of Christ's sufficiency.

DECLARATION
I LACK NOTHING.

24 HE MAKES ME LIE DOWN IN GREEN PASTURES.

LIE: THIS IS GOING TO BE A DISASTER.

He makes me lie down in green pastures.

PSALM 23:2

My friend Sarah hadn't returned my call in two days, and now anxiety gnawed at my sleep. She looked at me kind of funny a few days earlier, I recalled, which sent me tumbling down a rabbit hole of negative thoughts: *I probably said something that offended her. She probably doesn't want to be my friend anymore. She is probably badmouthing me to all of our other friends. They will probably abandon me too.*

The technical word for this spiral of negative thoughts about a theoretical future is called "catastrophizing." This irrational behavior occurs whenever we predict a negative outcome and allow our minds to run wild with dire possibilities.

For me, catastrophizing often creeps in at night when I'm alone with my thoughts. I begin to predict that Leif will die on his commute and leave me alone, that one of my friends will betray me, that my cancer will return and send me to an early grave.

We live in a culture laden with anxieties about the future. Anxiety lurks in our schools, our shopping malls, our movie theaters, our concert venues. The impact of this level of anxiety and fear surrounding our nation has yet to be fully calculated.

How do we find shalom, God's deep peace, in a world riddled with anxiety?

When I spent time with a shepherdess, I discovered that sheep are slow to lie down. They refuse to rest if they sense a menacing creature or hear any loud cracks of sound. If rams in the bunch are, well, *ram*bunctious, they'll remain standing, ready to bolt. And unless they're satiated, they'll keep wandering in search of food. When a good shepherd ensures all their needs are met, they lie in the field and rest.

THE GOOD SHEPHERD BANDAGES WOUNDS.

What keeps you up at night? Bad test results? A looming to-do list? Past-due notices? A nagging boss? Crippling loneliness? A cold war with a neighbor? A wayward child? You can drown under the weight of what-ifs. The Accuser shouts, "This is going to be a disaster."

The key to overcoming this lie is found in the fields. As the shepherd enters the pasture, the sheep's eyes fix on him. The sheep are wired to respond to the voice. The presence of the shepherd means they don't need to fret. They soon forget their worries, anxieties, fears. They lie down and rest.

The quality of a sheep's life depends on the character of the shepherd.

Skinny, sickly sheep are the reflection of a bad shepherd. Well-fed, protected sheep are the reflection of a good shepherd. A bad shepherd offers brown, arid desert and dirty streams. A good shepherd leads to verdant, lush pastures and fresh water.

A bad shepherd ignores the needs of the sheep. A good shepherd lays down his life for the sheep.

The Good Shepherd bandages wounds, attends to needs, and keeps his eyes on you—day and night. He bears your burdens, protects the gate, and tracks you down when you stray. The Good Shepherd's presence puts his sheep at ease.

So calm, sweet friend. Lie down and trust that the world rests firmly in the palm of God. No need to catastrophize or fall down a rabbit hole of negative ruminations. Allow the Good Shepherd to wrap his arms around you and baptize you in holy shalom.

DECLARATION
HE MAKES ME LIE DOWN
IN GREEN PASTURES.

25 HE LEADS ME BESIDE STILL WATERS.

LIE: I ALWAYS NEED TO DISTRACT MYSELF.

He leads me beside still waters.

PSALM 23:2 ESV

I recently joked with a friend as I reached for my smartphone that it's like a drug-laced Binky for grown-ups. I look to my phone when I'm bored, need a distraction, or want to feel better. Experts have compared personal technology use to an addictive hypodermic mechanism that delivers a digital drug. It promises stimulation and soothing every time, and it delivers—except when it doesn't.

Not all clicks and scrolls deliver the quick upper I want. Some lead to feelings of comparison, discouragement, and despair, which compel me to keep scrolling until I find good feelings again. Maybe you've noticed the same.

Electronic devices are a necessity for most of us. They help us communicate, shop, find our way, keep up with important news updates, and contact the police if we are in trouble. The issue is not with a particular device, game, or app, but the amount of time we engage with it and how we allow it to shape our minds, emotions, families, and capacity to flourish.

Those who overindulge in screen time experience increased levels of irritability, sleep disturbances, and poor concentration. Excess use is linked to anxiety, stress, and lower emotional stability. Plus, overuse can lead to the disintegration of friendships and even the family.

WHEN YOU QUIET THE PAIN, YOU CAN'T HEAR WHAT IT'S SAYING.

Maybe you too have bought into the Enemy's lie, "I always need to distract myself." Whether it's binge-watching a television show, shopping mindlessly, playing a favorite video game, or scrolling through an eternity of posts on social media, personal technology offers distraction in perpetuity.

Often, we reach for electronic devices to numb the pain inside. The only problem is, when you quiet the pain, you can't hear what it's saying or encounter healing.

Every human mind, without exception, needs opportunities to rest. If we deprive ourselves, our overstimulated brains grow tired, unable to process pain, boredom, and problems that need solving. Soon our minds can only focus on the task of locating the next distraction—and quick! Over time, this impacts individuals and the family unit as each person disengages from the others to focus on a technological interaction.

Christ invites us to step away from all distractions and encounter him, the one who heals our souls. It takes a lot of hard work to break old habits, but repetition will build new neural pathways, freeing us from these poisonous patterns.

In addition to leading us to green pastures where we can lie down in peace, the Good Shepherd "leads me beside still waters" (Psalm 23:2 ESV). Notice these aren't raging waters trying to take you away from where you are. These aren't rapids that can catch you off guard and lead to your demise. God wants to bring you to quiet waters, the kind that satisfy and rejuvenate, that ensure you're properly hydrated and strengthened for the day and the journey ahead. He longs to lead you away from the waves of agitation and clamor on your screen toward his peaceful, calm refreshment.

What changes do you need to make to break the electronic device addiction? Make a list of activities to do with your discretionary time that don't involve a screen. Take a walk and pray. Write a note of gratitude. Reflect on a scripture. Consider adding an app that limits your tech time. Turn off your notifications. Create tech-free zones in your home, such as the dinner table and bedroom. Set a time each week to go without technology and rediscover the still waters God has for you.

DECLARATION
HE LEADS ME
BESIDE STILL WATERS.

26 HE RESTORES MY SOUL.

LIE: IF I SLOW DOWN, I'LL FALL BEHIND.

He restores my soul.

PSALM 23:3 NKJV

When I was growing up, my parents never overtly pushed me to attain particular scores on tests or win athletic trophies. Instead, they prodded me with the words, "We only expect you to do your best."

It took me several decades and countless hours in a counselor's office as an adult to understand how these oft-used and well-meaning words caused harm. Namely, it's impossible to do one's best *all* the time in *every* endeavor. No single person contains the energy, the bandwidth, the ardor to live superlative at all times in all situations. Yet the Accuser whispers, "If you slow down, you'll fall behind," until every activity becomes a taskmaster demanding your finest efforts.

The drive toward productivity and success will exhaust you. Drivenness has a way of seeping into the ways you work and live and love and parent. It can even affect your relationship with God in the form of legalism. After all, if you slow down, you'll fall behind. The next thing you know, you're racing on a legalistic treadmill that requires you to keep working f-o-r-e-v-e-r. Soon faith is reduced to a list of dos and don'ts, a belief system that asks much and gives little, one that holds you to out-of-reach standards.

Jesus ushers us into a gentler, more joyful way of living. He invites all of us who are weary and burdened to come to him for rest (Matthew 11:28). Whenever you experience nagging guilt that you'll never do enough, you'll never work hard enough, and your best will never be good enough, Jesus responds with an invitation to experience his rest and restoration.

Are you working to the point of exhaustion? You're invited.
Are you weighed down with a heavy load? You're invited.
Are you feeling the pangs of fatigue and burnout? You're invited.

If you're feeling weary, great! You're the exact person Jesus is looking for. He awaits wide-armed for you to come. Yes, you. *Come to me*, he invites. *Come. To. Me.* If you answer the invitation, Jesus promises a 24-karat gift: refreshment.

The promise that the Good Shepherd will restore means he will "bring back." If the hard drive of your life becomes too full, you may need to delete some things before you can fully restore it to life. What would it feel like for your soul to be restored and refreshed by God?

"Take my yoke upon you and learn from me, for I am gentle and humble in heart, and you will find rest for your souls. For my yoke is easy and my burden is light" (Matthew 11:29–30). A yoke is a wooden frame that's stretched across the backs of a pair of animals. It enables them to pull heavy loads or plow a field. In the ancient world, a rabbi's interpretation of the Hebrew Scriptures became known as a yoke. In Matthew 11, in essence, Jesus says, "Trust my interpretation of God's law and

JESUS USHERS US INTO A GENTLER, MORE JOYFUL WAY OF LIVING.

take *my* yoke upon you"—an easy yoke with a light burden. If you adopt Jesus' way of living, you'll find more than a good night's sleep; you'll find rest for the core of your being.

Jesus doesn't relax God's standards. He offers a relationship through which you find the power to live into the fullness of truth, righteousness, holiness, and all that God intends. Best of all, you don't bear the yoke alone. He carries the heavy portion for you, alongside you.

The Savior always does the heavy lifting in your relationship with him. Instead of sweating to do your best in every situation, you can search for Christ in every situation and trust the work he's already doing. Take a deep breath and say yes to Jesus' invitation to rest and restore your weary soul.

DECLARATION
HE RESTORES MY SOUL.

27 GOD IS MY STRENGTH.

LIE: I AM A FRAUD.

The Lord is my strength and my shield; my heart trusts in him.

PSALM 28:7

The fear of public speaking paralyzed me for years. My stomach twisted and churned; sweat beads gathered on my upper lip; the muscles around my neck clenched me in their iron grip. This happened the day I taught for a crowd *and* for several days leading up to the event *and* for at least a week afterward. Before I stepped onstage, I'd make a panicky trot to the restroom with an upset stomach. After speaking, my body shook with tremors.

Whenever I spoke in front of an audience, regardless of the size, I felt as if I were putting my whole self out for the world to judge. No matter which outfit I wore, I still felt naked, vulnerable, see-through. I'd scan the lineup of other speakers and obsess about the much smarter, sharper, and stronger communicators.

> *She has a higher level of education.*
> *He has more striking insights and compelling stories.*
> *It's dumb luck that I'm here.*
> *People will eventually realize I'm a fraud.*

Have you ever had that feeling that it's only a matter of time before people find you out? The condition is so common that psychologists have given this behavior pattern a clinical name: impostor syndrome. An estimated 70 percent of Americans experience it at some point in their lives.[1]

- You tell yourself that you landed the job because the company was desperate, not because you're qualified. One day your boss is going to find out you've been googling all those right answers.
- You tell yourself that you're not as good a mom or dad as the others, and one day everyone will discover what a poor parent you are.
- You tell yourself that you're dating way out of your league, and you're certain that your significant other will realize it and leave.

Walking into situations where you feel like you're a fraud spikes stress and diminishes self-confidence.

I spent years living in agreement with the Accuser, believing that I was a fraud, and it took a heavy toll. I even thought I should stop speaking altogether. Then one day I sensed the Holy Spirit whisper, "All I'm calling you to do is this: you be you, and you be mine."

A wave of freedom crashed over my soul. God never asked me to be someone I was not. He asked me to be wholly his and wholly myself. In Christ, I had nothing to fear. As Psalm 28:7 says, "The Lord is my strength and my shield; my heart trusts in him." All I needed to do was own what was already true of both God and myself.

At the next speaking engagement, I slipped off my shoes, something that makes me feel most like myself. When my bare toes touched the stage, I declared, "God is my strength and shield. In him, I am strong and mighty." I still feel nervous sometimes, but nothing like before.

"YOU BE YOU, AND YOU BE MINE."

God is grounding me in the reality that I am neither impostor nor fraud—and neither are you.

Being wholly God's and wholly yourself will free you from the Accuser's lie that you're an impostor. You are no accident. Where God has placed you is no accident. What God has called you to do is no accident. You are not there because of dumb luck or because you're somehow undeserving. You're there because you've been handpicked by God. You are no more wholly yourself than when you are wholly God's.

Walk in boldness and confidence, O strong and mighty one. God's got your back.

DECLARATION
GOD IS MY STRENGTH.

28 GOD IS MY SHIELD.

LIE: THE WORLD IS A DANGEROUS, SCARY PLACE.

He is a shield to those who take refuge in him.

PROVERBS 30:5

I asked my friend Troy which prayer he wanted God to answer above all others. He said he wanted to be free of fear.

"I thought about praying for God to fix my problems, but I realized that I wouldn't be afraid for even five seconds, and the next problem would show up and I'd get afraid again," he explained. "I want to be free of fear because fear makes me miserable, and fear makes me do dumb things. Those dumb things make bad things worse."

Fear is one of the chief animating forces of the twenty-first century. We are afraid of the future, afraid of people who are unlike us, afraid of the alarming levels of violence and tragedy surrounding us. When news headlines read more like chapter titles in a dystopian novel, we may be tempted to agree with the Accuser, "The world is a dangerous, scary place."

Fear is a pack animal; it doesn't travel alone. Fear hangs out with anxiety, worry, and fret. When the frightening fraternity breaks down your door, chaos is quick to ensue. Trivial matters become seismic. Possibilities induce paralysis. You're tempted to shrink back from the big, beautiful life God intends for you.

Living fearless should be one of your top God-goals in life. God gives us this command far more often in the Bible than any other: "Do not be afraid!" A variation of this instruction appears 365 times, one mention for every day of the year. Perhaps this is a subtle hint that we must be reminded of this each day.

The Israelite leader Joshua received the charge to lead God's people into the promised land, a terrain filled with giants ready to wage war. God's response:

> As I was with Moses, so I will be with you; I will never leave you nor forsake you. *Be strong and courageous*, because you will lead these people to inherit the land I swore to their ancestors to give them. *Be strong and very courageous.*" (Joshua 1:5–7, emphasis added)

The Lord stood with Joshua as he stands with us. Notice the call: be strong and courageous. God repeats the instructions twice for emphasis.

How do you experience this strength and courage? Joshua 1:7–8 tips us off:

> Be careful to obey all the law my servant Moses gave you; do not turn from it to the right or to the left, that you may be successful wherever you go. Keep this Book of the Law always on your lips.

As Joshua's men prepare for battle, they sharpen their swords and steel themselves. But on the eve of preparations to conquer a kingdom, God reminds Joshua the true shield is found in words, not weapons. Power awaits in believing, speaking, sharing, and declaring the transformative truth of God's Word.

Why does this matter? When you acknowledge your fears in light of God's truth, you gain the confidence to move forward in spite of your fears, thus undoing fear's enslaving power.

LIVING FEARLESS SHOULD BE ONE OF YOUR TOP GOD-GOALS IN LIFE.

What if you were to make Joshua's promise yours? What if you awoke each day and, as you prepared to fight your battles, declared, "God is my refuge and strength!"? God's Word is flawless, and he remains a shield to everyone who takes refuge in him (Proverbs 30:5).

When we confess that God neither sleeps nor slumbers (Psalm 121:4), we ground ourselves in the truth that God is attentive to our every need. When we say God owns the cattle on a thousand hills (Psalm 50:10), we remember that all resources in the world rest at his disposal. When we share that every hair follicle on our heads is numbered (Matthew 10:30), we find comfort in knowing God pays attention to the fine details.

God is our shield, and nothing happens apart from his permission. As you make Joshua's declarations yours, you'll find strength for your struggles, and you'll enter the land of God's abundant promises.

DECLARATION
GOD IS MY SHIELD.

29 GOD IS ALWAYS WITH ME.

LIE: GOD IS NOWHERE TO BE FOUND.

"I am with you always."
MATTHEW 28:20

My friend Katie moved to the Democratic Republic of the Congo to work in microfinance, giving small loans and savings accounts to growing businesses. The extreme poverty, death from curable diseases, and lack of basic sanitation and food weighed heavy on her heart. Katie read passages of God's promises to those in need. Yet she witnessed a great disparity between the promise that the Lord will deliver the needy who cry out (Psalm 72:12) and the death toll in the Congo.

"Because of the widespread fraud and power grabbing from the nation's political and military leaders, I watched people—including single moms and children—cry out to God for help and still die from malnutrition," she said. "God promises to care, feed, and house his people, yet they remained unfed, unhoused. If God's promise to care for those in dire poverty seemed untrue, how could I believe in any of God's promises?"

Two years into her time in the Congo, Katie reached a crisis of faith, believing that God was nowhere to be found—for her and those she served. She thought about returning to her home in Virginia. But she knew that if she left at that low point, she might never get her faith back.

Katie remained in the Congo, fighting extreme poverty for the next year. "I started to engage in some unhealthy behavior," she said. "I started dating men who were harmful. That's when I knew I was in a dark place. Something had to change."

One morning she decided to attend church. While singing the lyrics to "How Great Is Our God," suddenly God was real again. "It's hard to explain," she says. "But I believed again. The Bible promises to feed the hungry and place widows in families. Though I didn't see that fulfillment around me, I knew God was present and true. Truer than my perception of whether and how He was fulfilling His promises."

JESUS PROMISES TO BE WITH YOU ALWAYS.

At the low point of her faith, Katie says it was as if God raised up the ground beneath her. "In the darkest of the dark, the most horrendous and heinous, God is still with us. And he calls us to be part of his great rescue plan."

Like Katie, sooner or later we will each experience a crisis of faith. In those situations, the Accuser wants you to question God and his promises. To make an agreement that God's words are untrustworthy. Or worse, that God is nowhere to be found. Yet Jesus promises to be with you always—in every moment, in every situation (Matthew 28:20).

In your low moments and crisis points, refuse to give in to the lie that God has abandoned you. When we proclaim, "Not today, Satan" and resist him, he will run away. "Resist the devil, and he will flee from you. Come near to God and he will come near to you" (James 4:7–8). There will come a day when you see God's faithfulness anew. He is with you and for you. No. Matter. What.

DECLARATION
GOD IS ALWAYS WITH ME.

30 GOD IS ALWAYS FOR ME.

LIE: THE OTHER SHOE IS ABOUT TO DROP.

This I know, that God is for me.

PSALM 56:9 NASB

In the late 1800s, New York City apartment buildings were designed so one bedroom stacked atop the next. The paper-thin ceilings meant you could hear your upstairs neighbor drop a shoe that had just been slipped off and then, a moment later, hear the drop of the other one. This familiar and sometimes annoying experience was repeated over and over again, providing the origin of the common expression "Waiting for the other shoe to drop."

Today the idiom describes the feeling of waiting for something to happen that seems inevitable and undesirable. All too often we find ourselves slipping into a waiting-for-the-other-shoe-to-drop mentality.

Maybe you've felt it too. You've been in a season of good health, but you tell yourself it can't last. Or you experience an influx of blessing and prosperity but tell yourself that one day it will all vanish. Or perhaps you resist intimacy with others because you're convinced they'll abandon you.

The Accuser wants you to live in fear of the other kerplunk. When you anticipate that events will turn sour, feelings of anxiety and fear take over. Studies show that 85 percent of the scenarios people worry about never end up happening.[1] In harboring these thoughts, you allow tomorrow's forecast of rain clouds to steal today's sunshine.

By encouraging your obsession about a future of negative events, the Accuser steals your joy and delight in the moment. You become less present to others, less grateful for the blessings before you. That's why God wants you to renounce this shoe-dropping mentality.

This lesson is easier said than implemented, as the ancient Israelites so clearly demonstrate. They stand in awe as their enemies' water turns to blood, hail crashes down on them from the sky, and darkness descends over the Egyptians' world, all while the Hebrews and their own firstborns are spared. God splits the Red Sea and allows the Israelites to cross safely, but then the water collapses and swallows Pharaoh's army. At every turn, God reveals himself to be sustainer, protector, and provider for the Israelites.

YOU DON'T HAVE TO WORRY ABOUT THE OTHER SHOE DROPPING.

Even so, once God's people safely escape Egypt, they hurl blistering accusations at God and at their human leader: Why did you bring us to this miserable place? Why have you brought us here to starve to death? What have you done? (Exodus 16:3).

Somewhere along the way, the Israelites begin to believe God is against them. That it is only a matter of time until they hear the thud of the other fallen shoe. But it never comes. God's display of miraculous power continues to sustain them in Egypt and in the wilderness as he reveals time and time again that he is *for* them.

God quenches their thirst from water out of a rock.
God nourishes their bellies with the sweet bread of heaven.
God protects them from the heat of the day and chills of night.
God delivers them victory after victory over their enemies.

Four decades after defying the laws of nature to lead the Hebrews out of slavery, God has to remind them of how much tender care he has displayed every step of the way: "During the forty years that I led you through the wilderness, your clothes did not wear out, nor did the sandals on your feet" (Deuteronomy 29:5). God wanted the Israelites to break free from their shoe-dropping mentality—and he wants us to break free too.

You don't have to worry about the other shoe dropping. You can trust in the One who travels with you and provides for you every step of the way. You can walk in the confidence that God is for you (Psalm

56:9). When you're not cowered under your bed, waiting for something negative to happen, you are free to live in the hope of new miracles arising all around you.

DECLARATION
GOD IS ALWAYS FOR ME.

31 GOD ALWAYS SEES ME.

LIE: I AM INVISIBLE.

For the eyes of the LORD range throughout the earth to strengthen those whose hearts are fully committed to him.

2 CHRONICLES 16:9

Several years ago, I had the opportunity to have dinner with one of my Christian heroes and her husband. I bubbled with excitement all day, imagining everything I would learn, the ways I would be challenged, the opportunity to learn about hands-on ministry. The dinner didn't fall on any ordinary day by chance-in-stance; it happened to be my birthday. While I'd been promised that detail would be kept under wraps, I knew it was going to be the perfect ending to a day of celebration.

Leif and I arrived at the restaurant fifteen minutes early. When the couple appeared, I ran over to greet my hero with a huge bear hug. She introduced me to her husband, and we soon settled down for a full-course meal. I peppered her with questions, and she graciously answered. But from time to time she deferred to her husband to answer. Whenever I followed up with a question to him, he didn't respond.

At first, I wondered if he were hard of hearing, and I looked to my husband quizzically. Leif stepped in and repeated the question. That time the husband responded. But as he spoke, he looked only at my husband, not me. This pattern repeated itself throughout the evening with ever-increasing awkwardness. Leif did his best to grace over the oddity during conversation, but slowly I slipped into the background, an empty wallflower on display.

To this man, I wasn't worth a response. My question, my voice, my presence didn't matter. I was invisible. I left the dinner heartbroken and cried myself to sleep.

Few things can cut as deeply in the soul as being invisible. We come into this world as infants looking for a face—any face—that will see us, recognize us, show us love. When that love isn't there, whether as a child or as an adult, we find ourselves with the dull ache of a universal unmet need.

Maybe you, too, have been around people who make you feel barely noticeable or like an outcast, stirring feelings of rejection and worthlessness. Perhaps you are naturally shy or tend to be the quiet one at gatherings, and you leave wondering if it mattered that you were there at all. Or you used to turn heads when you strolled down the sidewalk, but now your youthful beauty has faded. You can barely get someone to open a door for you. In those moments, it's easy to wonder, *Am I here? Do I really exist? Does anyone see me?*

That's when the Accuser whispers, "You are invisible. You're neither worthy nor worth it."

Yet nothing could be further from the truth. The Scripture confirms that in every situation, every moment, God sees you. There's not a board room or classroom or living room in which his eyes are not on you.

IN EVERY SITUATION, EVERY MOMENT, GOD SEES YOU.

If anyone in the Bible would feel invisible, it's Hagar, an Egyptian slave and handmaid who serves Abraham and Sarah. In this couple's desperate desire for a child, they agree that Abraham should sleep with Hagar and impregnate her. Once the baby is on the way, Abraham and Sarah don't even see Hagar as human. Sarah mistreats her. Not once do they even speak her name. Hagar runs for her life into the wilderness, and God meets her there. Not only does the angel of God call Hagar by name; he shows loving interest in her by asking where she's come from and where she's going. God promises her the very same thing he has promised Abraham: her descendants will be too numerous to count.

Then Hagar uses a striking expression afforded to no one else. She names the God who has spoken to her *El Roi*, which means "the God who sees me." She is utterly astounded that he has seen her, noticed her, cared about her. And that gives her the hope she needs to go on.

Like Hagar in the desert, you, too, can know El Roi, the God who sees you. No matter the room you find yourself in, no matter the gathering you attend, no matter the person you sit across from—even if it's your birthday—you are not invisible to God. He sees you.

DECLARATION
GOD ALWAYS SEES ME.

32 NO WEAPON FORMED AGAINST ME WILL PROSPER.

LIE: I'LL ALWAYS BE A VICTIM.

No weapon formed against you shall prosper.

ISAIAH 54:17 NKJV

When I was diagnosed with an aggressive cancer, my mind raced: *What's the treatment plan? How will my body respond? How quickly can I recover from chemotherapy?* I resisted only one question: *Why me?*

When crisis crashes into your life, it's easy to ask why you have been dealt this hand. But asking the "why me?" question rarely leads to restoration or healing. The Enemy often uses this question to reinforce the lie "You'll always be a victim."

Psychologists warn against the corrosiveness of a victim mentality, in which people define themselves by a negative experience or circumstance. While we must acknowledge how we have been victimized by oppressive people, terrible events, or horrific acts, the victim mentality forces us to redefine our identity. We transition from a person who has experienced something awful into a victim above all else.

Why is the victim mentality so dangerous?

For one, it can convince people to adopt a permanent "poor me" attitude. They become convinced that life is beyond their control and others are out to deliberately cause harm. They catastrophize and excessively worry, forfeiting their sense of security and joy. Taking on a victim mentality will lead you into blaming others, filing constant complaints, and throwing world-class pity parties. Beyond this, a victim mentality will steal your power because you'll cede your responsibility and right to define yourself.

A VICTIM MENTALITY WILL STEAL YOUR POWER.

The Enemy wants you to believe you are nothing more than a victim, and you'll always be one, because then you'll be neutralized as a child of God. Your gifts will be stifled as you redirect your energy into the poor-me mindset. You won't have to take responsibility for anything. You'll become the kingpin in the blame game. You'll likely feel interesting or important as you share your stories. You'll enjoy the attention of people who feel sorry for you. This can then become a pathway to manipulate or control others as they attempt to care for you. No wonder the lie "You'll always be a victim" is so prevalent!

Here are a few signs you may have come into agreement with this untruth:

- You're suspicious of others' intentions despite a lack of evidence.
- You always blame others when life doesn't go your way.
- You share your tragic stories, often repeatedly to the same people.
- You allow your thoughts to be ruled by pessimism and negativity.
- You surround yourself with those who also blame, point fingers, and find fault.[1]

Once you've fully processed a traumatic event with a professional counselor, you can break the victim mentality by shifting your focus from the crisis to Christ, from the problem to the Person with the power to carry you through.

Daily declarations combined with prayer can help set you free. My cancer diagnosis did not surprise God, and knowing that God is good, God is with me, and God is for me meant that even in the midst of the pain and suffering, God was still at work.

One day you, too, will find yourself on the front lines of a battlefield you never chose. In that moment, remember the declaration of the prophet Isaiah: "'No weapon forged against you will prevail, and you will refute every tongue that accuses you. This is the heritage of the servants of the LORD" (Isaiah 54:17).

The Enemy says, "Once a victim, always a victim," but you don't have to align yourself with the Accuser's voice. Listen for God's voice in his Word and in good counsel. God is your champion. Your heritage from the Lord is to be victorious, and he provides your vindication. You will rise above and refute the tongue of the Enemy. You are more than a victim. As God's own, you are a victor, and your name is victorious.

DECLARATION
NO WEAPON FORMED AGAINST ME WILL PROSPER.

33 I AM ANOINTED.

"The Spirit of the Lord is on me, because he has
anointed me to preach good news to the poor."
LUKE 4:18 CSB

My throat tightens. Fear races down my spine like an electric current.
My mind spins like a broken sprinkler head. I want to share my faith,
but I can't find the right words. Or the courage to speak them. I wonder if this is the proper time, if it will make things weird, or if I'll be
asked a follow-up question for which I don't know the answer.

Even after a lifetime in ministry, sharing my faith one-on-one is scary.
That's why sometimes I don't say anything at all.

One of the most devious schemes of the Enemy is getting us to believe
the lie that we can't share our faith. Yet the good news of Jesus is too
good to keep to ourselves, and we have been anointed to spread it all
over the globe.

I rediscovered this on a recent adventure to Croatia, where I helped a
family on a remote island to bring in an olive harvest.[1] Sometimes we

worked ten hours a day. My arms, shoulders, and hamstrings grew sore and knotted. In the process of picking, I received many small cuts on my hands from the branches. But when I returned back to our home each night, my hands looked like they'd been soaking in luxurious and expensive oils at a world-class spa.

God designed olives, their oil, and even their branches with antibacterial and antioxidant properties. As your hands busily work with olives, you experience their healing nature firsthand, soaking right into your skin. But while you're doing the work, you may not notice it at all.

The anointing with oil, throughout the Bible, symbolizes the power of the Holy Spirit being given to a person for a designated task. Moses anoints Aaron for the priesthood (Exodus 29:1– 9). Samuel is instructed to anoint kings. When Saul is anointed, the Spirit of the Lord comes on him in power marked by prophesying (1 Samuel 10:1–10). All those anointed are called to bring healing to the land. When Jesus arrives among the Israelites, healing surges through his presence. *Messiah* means "Anointed One," and Christ brings healing to the land through the good news he proclaims.

YOU, TOO, HAVE BEEN ANOINTED.

In Luke 4:18–19, Jesus quotes from Isaiah: "The Spirit of the Lord is on me, because he has anointed me to proclaim good news to the poor.

He has sent me to proclaim freedom for the prisoners and recovery of sight for the blind, to set the oppressed free, to proclaim the year of the Lord's favor." That's true healing.

The same Spirit of the Lord and the same anointing to preach good news that rests on Jesus rests on you. You, too, have been anointed. That's the last thing the Adversary wants you to believe. Instead, he wants to shove you into a silent grave, to convince you that you don't have anything to offer. He doesn't want you to remember that Christ's healing power and presence flow through you. As a child of God, you are a spiritual powerhouse of liberation and healing everywhere you go to set captives free, to restore others physically and emotionally, to usher in the wonders of God's kingdom.

I do not know in what circumstance, with which person, at what time you believe you cannot share your faith. Yet you are God's living testimony, anointed with the power of the Holy Spirit to bring good news everywhere you go.

DECLARATION
I AM ANOINTED.

34 I AM EMPOWERED.

LIE: WOMEN DON'T DO THAT.

"You will receive power when the Holy Spirit comes on you; and you will be my witnesses in Jerusalem, and in all Judea and Samaria, and to the ends of the earth."
ACTS 1:8

After I spoke at a leadership conference a few years ago, a man cornered me in the hallway with a rather pointed question: "What gives you the right, as a woman, to stand up and speak to this audience, which includes men, about anything having to do with Scripture?"

The question stole my breath. The Spirit stirred inside me. Before I could process my response, I answered, "Because I am God's daughter."

The man looked at me, recognizing the principle that a daughter—whether on behalf of a heavenly Father or a human one—has the right to speak for the family. The stony look on his face melted, and he said, "That's a good answer."

Perhaps you've been tempted to believe the lie "Women don't do that!" when you step out in your gifts, activate your talents, share your insights. Maybe those words have been spoken, aloud or silently, over your profession, your dreams, your nonprofit. Or maybe you feel called to stay home full-time to care for the kids, but in a double-income culture, people keep telling you, "Women don't do that anymore."

This insidious lie falls like a gavel. It renders a verdict on your life by attacking a part of you that you can't change.

Before you were a bead of sweat on your mother's forehead, you were given a destiny. The word *destiny* comes from the Latin root meaning to "make firm" or "establish."

YOU WERE GIVEN A DESTINY.   In other words, you have a God-given destination that's prepared for you. If you believe the naysayers who huff, "Women don't do that!" then you won't lay claim to all God has for you.

Consider for a moment some of the women of the Bible who rose up and refused to believe those who said, "Women don't do that!"

- Esther, ready to rescue the Jewish people, who enters the king's presence without an invitation. Everyone knows people—and especially women—don't barge into the throne room and speak their minds.
- Rahab, who risks her life to save the Hebrew spies. Surely women don't assume that kind of high-stakes activism.

- Deborah, who serves ancient Israel as a judge, prophet, and military leader. After all, how could a woman hold such high offices?
- Mary, who becomes pregnant by the Holy Spirit out of wedlock. That's out-of-bounds for any female.
- The woman who soaks Jesus' feet with her tears and expensive perfume. How dare a woman touch a man in public—and in such an intimate way.
- Those women who gather at the empty tomb. They're sent by Jesus to preach the good news of his resurrection to the disciples, another thing "women don't do."

Through their obedience and the power of the Holy Spirit, these women save nations, rescue God's people, welcome the Messiah, prepare Christ for his burial, and introduce the world to the gospel of Jesus Christ.

We can't afford to have gifted women sidelined by the lie that we "aren't supposed to do that"—especially at this moment in history. We need you launching nonprofits to save the world. Guiding companies to make ethical, God-honoring decisions. Raising up mighty children who love Jesus. Transforming local communities one person at a time. Introducing others to the superabundance of grace found in Jesus Christ.

Gifted and empowered: this is who you are. Boldly walk in the fullness of all God has for you.

DECLARATION
I AM EMPOWERED.

35 I AM CALLED TO REACH PEOPLE FAR FROM GOD.

LIE: I AM ASHAMED.

For I am not ashamed of the gospel, because it is the power of God that brings salvation to everyone who believes.

ROMANS 1:16

Imagine a man with muscles so strong he snaps iron chains with a twitch. He roams at night, shouting profanities in an otherworldly voice. Children flee from his presence; women avert their eyes; his family likely disowns him.

That's the tortuous existence of the man plagued by demons. In darkness, he crawls through the cemetery; in shadows, he retreats to the wild. All the while, he slashes his wrists, his legs, his face. He's the strongest man in town, Mark tells us, and no one is powerful enough to subdue him (Mark 5:4).

Nothing can stop this man—except Jesus. Only the Savior possesses the spiritual muscle and keys to freedom. With a few syllables from Jesus' mouth, a hoard of unclean spirits rush from his body and enter roaming swine. The man's mind clears, and he changes into clean clothes.

When Jesus waves bon voyage, the man begs to climb aboard the boat. It's hard to blame him, considering all the shame he must carry from years of unruly behavior. Embarrassed by his actions, he likely feels self-conscious, tempted toward self-blame. No wonder he tries to leave with his liberator.

Shame is a powerful force in our lives. Sometimes, like the man plagued by unclean spirits, we feel shame arise from an intense period of public humiliation. Often, it emerges from a deep sense that we are defective and unfixable. When conscience or guilt says, "I have done something bad," shame takes the leap to proclaim, "I *am* bad."

The Accuser will always try to convince you that something is wrong with you and you should be ashamed. He wants you to believe this lie, to make this agreement. When you think the problem is within you—that the problem *is* you—you'll start pulling away from God and others until you're isolated. Sometimes it's easier to recognize this truth in a chained madman than in ourselves.

What are you most ashamed of? Maybe you cheated on your spouse. Perhaps you spoke harshly to a parent, never realizing those would be the last words they heard. Maybe you stole money from a business partner and concluded that forgetting about it was less painful than fessing up. Maybe it was an honest mistake.

Whatever the source of your shame or regret, Jesus embraced the cross to defeat it once and for all. If your shame comes as the result of sin, you can repent and find sweet forgiveness. If your regret is from a mistake or poor decision, Jesus' forgiveness is readily available for that too.

> JESUS EMBRACED THE CROSS TO DEFEAT IT ONCE AND FOR ALL.

But even after you receive God's grace, you may still find yourself clinging to the shame, trying to hide in the shadows. Sometimes breaking free from shame and regret and living in forgiveness require exposure and vulnerability. They require telling your story within a community of trusted confidants and, eventually, testifying about the good news of the miracle to others who don't know that God can bring them freedom too.

Jesus instructs the once-possessed man to stay. He urges the man to return to his people with a two-prong mission: first, tell them the jaw-dropping miracles God has done in your life, and second, tell them how he has had compassion on you. Jesus transformed the man's story from a source of shame and regret into a beautiful instrument of God's glory.

He can transform yours too.

Whenever you feel shame rising, whether from a past mistake or a present pattern, the natural tendency is to hide. Board a boat and sail away. Keep your story under wraps. But this only gives the shame more power. Instead, rejoice in the freedom of having been forgiven and set free from the prison of shame. Share the great things God has done for you and how he's had compassion on you (2 Timothy 1:7–8). Proclaim it boldly. Tell your story. The world is dying to hear it.

DECLARATION
I AM CALLED TO REACH
PEOPLE FAR FROM GOD.

36 MY WORDS HAVE POWER.

The tongue has the power of life and death.
PROVERBS 18:21

Leif started singing a song over me soon after we were married. This was no ordinary tune. The refrain lacked melody, harmony, rhyme. Perhaps it wasn't a song at all. Well, except to me.

We were newlyweds in our late twenties. We felt late to the marriage game back then, which seems silly now, but the social stigma was real. Leif was the oldest of three brothers and the last to marry. We both experienced the pressure of always being a bridesmaid or groomsman but never a bride or groom. Grandmother told me every Valentine's Day that I was an old maid. I think she meant well.

Leif had $19,479 in student loans, and I refused to marry him unless he became debt-free. (Dave Ramsey would have been proud.) Leif soon found a better-paying job, moved back in with his parents, rode a bike to cut fuel costs, and worked overtime. Nine months later, we were wed.

The first year of marriage abounded with joy—and tears. We discovered our communication skills were a lot like our bank account: zilch-a-mundo. Navigating our new lives together took hard work. From the kitchen to the bathroom counter (which I commandeered) to the bedroom, each space required discussion, negotiation, renegotiation. Sometimes the tears flowed so hot and heavy that I wondered if we'd survive it.

Leif mastered the fine art of pulling me out of my despair. When I spiraled, he wrapped his arms around me in a bear hug and whispered in my ear . . .

> *I'm never letting go. I love you. I picked you, and I'm so grateful you picked me. Your saying yes is the best thing that's ever happened to me. I'm the luckiest man in the whole world.*

This melody-less song became Leif's ballad to me. He has been singing it ever since. I soon learned the chorus . . .

> *I love my life with you. Thank you so much for picking me. There's no one I'd rather live this life with.*

As we inch toward two decades of marriage, we no longer wait for the hard or sad or mad to whisper these words. We sing them in the morning with sleep crusties in the corners of our eyes and in the evening after a brutal day's work. The song has become a prayer of thanksgiving and joy and delight. The words we speak to each other, about each other, over each other make a difference. Our words have power.

My friend Cindy chats it up with me when we're one-on-one, but she becomes the quiet one at dinner parties. Cindy doesn't speak up in mixed company because she believes she doesn't have anything important to contribute. My friend Tom says that he has strong opinions about how his company could be run more efficiently, but he hasn't said anything because "no one will listen."

SING A SONG OF THANKSGIVING AND BLESSING OVER THOSE YOU LOVE MOST.

Maybe you let other people make decisions for you and fail to express your opinions because you, too, have made an agreement with the Accuser: "What I have to say doesn't matter."

The Scripture reminds us that life and death are in the power of the tongue (Proverbs 18:21). If you think your words don't have power, recall a time when the words spoken to you altered the course of your life. Maybe the simple encouragement of "You can do this!" from a teacher or coach gave you the strength to apply for college or launch your business. We all have stories like this, subtle reminders that words have the power to renew relationships, rekindle love, and revive hearts.

Today sing a song of thanksgiving and blessing over those you love most.

But before I go, may I sing a songlet over you?

You are a gift. You bring others such joy. The world is better because of your love and generosity. You help others in ways you don't even realize by simply being you. Your words have power. Use them well.

DECLARATION
MY WORDS HAVE POWER.

37 I WILL LOOK FOR EVERY OPPORTUNITY TO SPEAK LIFE.

LIE: I ALWAYS HAVE TO GET THE LAST WORD.

The soothing tongue is a tree of life.
PROVERBS 15:4

I can't believe she said that! I'm going to give her a piece of my mind!

My keyboard smoked as I typed hard and fast a message to communicate her foolishness, her mistake, and how much damage she had caused with her latest political post on Instagram. I made sure that by the time she was done reading my words, she'd feel sick to her stomach. I added an extra portion of guilt for good measure and then hit Send.

I stomped off to tell Leif how right I was and how wrong she was. My husband's eyes closed as he rested his chin on his chest.

"What's the matter?" I asked.

"That's the last thing she needs right now," he said. "Her child is in the hospital, and it's not widely known yet, but she's going through a divorce."

Now I was the one who felt ill. I raced back to the computer to take down my comment, but it was too late. She'd already posted a counterattack, one uglier and more personal. It took everything in me not to respond, not to get the last word. My fingers fired like jackhammers, but reflecting on her pain, I deleted the post and walked away.

SOME WORDS ARE BETTER LEFT UNSAID.

I'm not the only one who believes the Enemy's lie that it's best to get the last word. I mean, if you get the final word, then you win the argument, right? And if you win the argument, that makes you a winner, right?

I've learned the hard way that you can win the argument and lose the relationship. Because trouncing with the last word can erode feelings of trust and the sense that you're playing fair. Some words are better left unsaid.

We've all lost ourselves in the furor of an argument. Possessed by our emotions and pride, we speak too soon, say too much, or speak words we don't really mean. We talk before we think. We blurt an answer before hearing the whole question. Worse, we often speak the harshest words to those we most love.

Early in our marriage, both Leif and I just had to get the last word, and it took a toll on both of us. Miscommunication and misunderstanding multiplied like bad debt with exorbitant interest.

I struggled to let issues go. I would say I forgave him, but I still harbored animosity. I prayed for God to give me wisdom on how to let go and move on, but that didn't keep me from pouting for days on end.

First Peter 3:9 instructs us never to "repay evil with evil or insult with insult." On the contrary, we are to repay evil with blessing. Every time we do, we inherit a blessing.

I took this passage to heart. Leif and I developed a simple practice. If one of us felt that we'd offended through word or deed, that person would ask, "Will you forgive me?" The other person could offer forgiveness on the spot or after a while because—let's be honest—sometimes you need a second or two to cool down.

As soon as the person offended said, "Yes, I forgive you," the offender had to speak three heartfelt compliments about the other person. "I appreciate your sense of humor." "I love the way you encourage people."

"I like snuggling with you." The act of blessing or being blessed melted our hearts. Any lingering anger soon vanished.

One of the most powerful spiritual practices you can implement is forfeiting your right to have the final word in a conflict. You can speak blessings and life over everyone you encounter. Declare right now that you will be a blessing, not a burden, and let it be the final word for you today.

DECLARATION
I WILL LOOK FOR EVERY OPPORTUNITY TO SPEAK LIFE.

38 I WILL SHOW COMPASSION.

When Jesus landed and saw a large crowd, he had
compassion on them and healed their sick.
MATTHEW 14:14

What behaviors in people most annoy you?

> The checkout person moving at a snail's pace?
> The motorist driving fifteen miles per hour below the speed
>   limit?
> The family member who turns every discussion political?
> The adult children who refuse to clean up after themselves?
> The person you sent a gift who can't be bothered to say
>   thank you?

The type of behavior that makes me want to scream is when a person
talks incessantly and never takes a breath. You know, the person who
doesn't realize that a conversation requires two people who both have
a chance to share something about themselves. These are the people
I try to avoid.

We all have our pet peeves, and they aren't always rational. It's so easy to confuse the behavior of a person with the actual person, until we almost forget they are human.

In moments of frustration, the Accuser tries to reclassify the people we're interacting with into problems by getting us to make a powerful agreement: "That person is a problem." The Enemy loves to dehumanize, to encourage us to forget that every human is an image bearer of God.

"He's a problem child."

"That's a problem employee."

"She's always been a problem."

Christ calls us to break this agreement and instead look on others with soft eyes. What are soft eyes? Diana Butler Bass, author of *Grateful: The Transformative Power of Giving Thanks*, describes the choice to view others with soft eyes as the capacity to see them more broadly and view the entire picture. This means seeing beyond the behavior and into the heart and situation of the person.[1]

Jesus demonstrates this through his abundant displays of compassion. Because of his soft eyes, sick people are healed, corpses breathe life, and a fellow cross-sufferer receives forgiveness. Each act demonstrates that, through Christ, we can become more than a *type*—a blind man, some dead guy, another criminal. Through Christ we, Bartimaeus, Lazarus, and the one promised paradise are beloved children whose names rest on God's lips.

> SOFT EYES CALL US TO A MORE COMPASSIONATE VIEW OF OTHERS.

After receiving the news of John the Baptist's death, Jesus and his disciples retreat to a quiet place to rest. The crowd tracks down Jesus like a bloodhound. Exhausted and grieving, Jesus could easily assess the people as burdensome; instead, he looks on them with compassion and heals everyone who is sick (Matthew 14:14).

The word *compassion* consists of two Latin root words, *com*, meaning "with," and *passio*, meaning "suffering." To have compassion is to resist the impulse to dismiss others as a problem and instead enter into others' pain.

Looking on others with soft eyes calls us to a more compassionate view of others . . .

- to remember the checkout person is likely overworked and underpaid
- to remember the slow driver may have a medical condition

- to remember the partisan family member may be acting out of fear or anger
- to remember the people who don't offer help may be weary too
- to remember we all forget to say thank you from time to time
- to remember people cannot give us what they do not have

Ephesians 4:29 instructs us to avoid corrupting talk and use our words to build up and extend grace to those who hear. You don't have to excuse others' bad behavior to give them the benefit of the doubt, unmerited grace, an encouraging word, an extra helping of compassion. Today practice looking at others with soft eyes and seeing the image of God in everyone you meet.

DECLARATION
I WILL SHOW COMPASSION.

39 I WILL BRING OUT THE BEST IN OTHERS.

LIE: I'M BETTER OFF ALONE.

Bring out the best in others in a conversation.
COLOSSIANS 4:6 THE MESSAGE

My family moved around a lot when I was a kid—from Cocoa Beach, Florida; to Maggie Valley, North Carolina; to Steamboat Springs, Colorado. We also lived for several years aboard a boat, sailing from one remote island to another. Let's just say I had quite the childhood.

Without siblings, I learned to occupy myself with books and made-up games. I longed for connection with other children, but sometimes the places were isolated, and there wasn't much opportunity. I withdrew into myself.

My seventh-grade teacher asked me to stay after class one day. She had noticed I'd become withdrawn. Bluntly, she asked if I was suicidal. At twelve years old, I had never contemplated taking my life. Heck, I didn't even know anyone who had taken their own life. The question proved so jarring that it jolted me into considering my social behavior.

Somewhere along the way—after experiencing letdown after letdown—I'd grown tired of making the effort to befriend others. Looking back now, I realize I'd embraced the false belief "I'm better off alone." I was the only person I could count on to never let me down.

I wish this tempting false belief was limited to childhood, but it can slip into our lives at any age. Maybe after the divorce, you thought, *I'm better off alone.* Or after the heartbreak, *I'm better off alone.* Or after the betrayal, *I'm better off alone.* Or after those you loved moved away, *I'm better off alone.*

This is one of the most harmful agreements you can make because it severs you from life-giving friendship, connection, and love—all essential human needs. If the pandemic revealed anything, it's how much we need each other. If the Accuser can isolate you, he will disconnect you, then work double time to defeat you.

You are *never* better off alone. Did you hear me? *Never!*

God handcrafted you for community. He demonstrates this by living in rich relationship himself (Genesis 1:26). Father, Son, and Holy Spirit reside in trinitarian fellowship, celebrating one another as they celebrate you. God is communal, and as humans made in God's image, we are too.

In the second chapter of Genesis, God looks on Adam and declares that it's no *bueno* for the man to be alone (2:18). God fashions for Adam a helper, a best friend, a companion, Eve.

The Creator crafts us to experience vibrant relationships. The church is supposed to be a body where all the parts fulfill their intended purposes and where the differences in those purposes are respected, valued, and encouraged. Stepping out to build new friendships feels risky, but it's also rewarding.

Today become intentional about building friendships. Look for those God is bringing into your life who speak life and hope and share similar values. Courageously invite new people into your life. Use your words to bring out the best in others, both offline and online, rather than put them down or cut them out (Colossians 4:6).

YOU ARE *NEVER* BETTER OFF ALONE.

Now, not everyone is going to be your new BFF. Some people are meant to intersect your life for a short season and no more. But God has not forgotten you, and he has people for you to grow and connect with. How can you be sure of this? Because it's in community that you experience healthy connections that affirm your gifts, your talents, your calling, and your value to others and to God.

Furthermore, it's in community that you can help *others* discover the riches and beauty God has instilled in them. You are created to be a life-giving friend who brings out the best in others. Declare that truth each day from whatever table, hostel, hotel room, or pew where you find yourself.

DECLARATION
I WILL BRING OUT
THE BEST IN OTHERS.

40 SHAME IS NOT MY MASTER.

LIE: NO ONE CAN EVER KNOW.

Anyone who believes in him will never be put to shame.
ROMANS 10:11

My friend Lily spent more than forty years of her life never telling a soul that her father had sexually abused her as a child. She held the secret tight and deep and promised herself that the truth would never see the light of day. As the years passed, the weight of her secret and her unwillingness to confide in anyone became unbearable. She drank bottles of chardonnay to numb the pain. She took antianxiety medication to cool the embers of increasing panic attacks. She slipped deeper into depression.

Her vow to hide her secret was killing her inside. She needed to drag the truth into the light. Lily was terrified of telling anyone, until she found herself in a counselor's office, disintegrated into a teary mess. The words poured out of her with velocity—every last traumatic detail.

"I walked out lighter and freer than I'd ever been," Lily says. "I still had so much work to do, understanding and healing and forgiving, but bringing my secret into the light made all the difference."

One of the most destructive agreements we can make is "No one can ever know." The Accuser tries to convince us that our shame, our secret, our struggle is better left unspoken. He warns us to craft a mask that makes it seem like we have it all together when, in reality, we're unraveling inside.

Sorry, but time does not heal all wounds. God does. And he does it with light.

Four words launch the greatest story ever told: *In the beginning, God . . .* On that first day, God could have chosen anything to be his first creation, but do you know what topped his to-do list? Light (Genesis 1:3). God fashions radiance. From nothingness, with mere syllables, he unleashes his sudden, breathtaking, illuminating power. Now flash forward to the end of the story, or rather the new beginning, and guess what God does? He eliminates all traces of darkness *forever* (Revelation 22:5).

Throughout Scripture, light continues to signal the presence of God. The psalmist describes the light of God's face (Psalm 4:6), and Isaiah describes God as an "everlasting light" (Isaiah 60:19–20). When

Christ arrives on earth, he reveals that he has come as light into the world so those who believe are no longer in darkness (John 12:46).

Even nature displays the power of light. Plants left in the darkness fade; when brought into the light, they grow and thrive.

HEALING COMES FROM THE ONE WHO IS LIGHT.

Bright light therapy is effective against certain types of depression and sleep disorders, and many doctors believe red light therapy promotes wound healing and tissue repair.

Why is God so concerned with illumination? Because darkness is the Accuser's domain. Our Enemy operates best in the dark, convincing us it's the safest place to keep our awful secrets, our past horrors, and our worst choices. Keep it in the dark, and we won't have to feel the pain we've suffered—or worse, the pain we've inflicted on others.

The Enemy of our souls works overtime to keep us in the dark—to keep us from discovering that healing comes from the One who is Light.

Christ's radiance destroys darkness and its power. Though once in darkness, you are now the light of Christ. Go forth and live as a child of light (Ephesians 5:8). Lily lives free today because she trusted this powerful truth. You can too.

The One who created light, who spun the stars and carved the moon, handcrafted you to experience the light of the world, Jesus Christ, so you no longer have to be held hostage to shame.

DECLARATION
SHAME IS NOT MY MASTER.

41 GOD'S POWER IS PERFECTED IN MY VULNERABILITY.

LIE: I NEED TO HIDE MY WEAKNESSES.

"[God's] power is made perfect in weakness."
2 CORINTHIANS 12:9

Most of us are skilled at hiding our shortcomings, but when we gather around the table, our warts have a way of popping up.

If you don't believe me, recall your last Thanksgiving meal or digital online gathering. Can you recount a story of someone who said something so awkward, no one knew how to respond? The family member who kicked off a political debate nobody wanted? The friend whose offhand comments lacerated you?

The table has a way of unmasking us. Sharing a meal reveals our imperfections and woundedness. One of the most frequent themes in the New Testament is mealtime. If you look closely at these breakfasts, lunches, and dinners where Christ is present, you uncover a pattern pointed out by author Eugene Peterson:

BLESSED + BROKEN + GIVEN

All three elements are on display. Peterson says they are "the shape of the Eucharist . . . the shape of the Gospel . . . the shape of the Christian."[1] We experience the fullness of life when we are reshaped this way. We are blessed, broken, and given together in Christ.

God blesses you through the food. When you come to the table with gratitude for this blessing, you also bring your whole self—all your unique strengths, talents, and gifts alongside your weaknesses and wounds. As you let down your guard and allow your tablemates to truly see and experience who you are in Christ, they receive yet another *blessing*. Through your honesty about your *brokenness*, you *give* them a rare gift: yourself. They then experience the freedom to be real about their own brokenness, and something mysterious happens: you are all made whole.

The table is more than a place where hungry people gather to eat; it's a place where broken people gather to belong. Touched by the blessings of God in the food and in each other, we are called to give our whole selves, not a varnished version, to those alongside us.

The Accuser's lie is that we must hide our weaknesses. Table fellowship—whether in person or digitally—has the power to break this lie because Christ presides there.

This pattern of blessed + broken + given we experience around the table is meant to train us to replicate the same pattern in our everyday lives. All too often we're tempted to cover up our weaknesses, mask our imperfections, and camouflage our failings. Christ calls us to vulnerability. At the Last Supper, he gives a new command; that we love one another (John 13:34).

YOU ARE MADE WHOLE.

Author Brené Brown defines vulnerability as "uncertainty, risk, and emotional exposure."[2] It's what happens when we quite literally bare our souls to one another in a safe space. Brown suggests that vulnerability sits at the center of all meaningful human experiences. Without it, we rob ourselves of so many other important virtues:

Without vulnerability, we struggle to be connected.
Without vulnerability, we struggle to be compassionate.
Without vulnerability, we struggle to be courageous.

One of the greatest portraits of vulnerability in human history is Jesus. Born as a helpless infant, he chose to set aside heavenly glory to become fragile human flesh. He refused to fight back when placed on trial. To become vulnerable is to become Christlike. To offer all of who we are to anyone who needs it is to look more like Jesus. After all, God's power is perfected in our weakness (2 Corinthians 12:9).

When you refuse to pretend you're flawless, you open the floodgates to God's power in your life. The path to vulnerability is not for the weak-kneed. It requires sharing what you'd rather hide and—even more frightening—sitting in uncertainty. Vulnerability never promises a guaranteed outcome. Will you be accepted or rejected? Harmed or healed? Pull up a chair at the table if you want to find out.

At mealtimes, gathered among people I trust and God's presence, the table becomes a safe space. It's the place I share my fears of being a failure or fraud. The place I speak my audacious dreams that I may never achieve. The place I confess my secrets and pain.

Sit down, be the blessing you are, break bread, give yourself to your tablemates by being vulnerable about your brokenness, and watch God's power perfected right before your eyes.

DECLARATION
GOD'S POWER IS PERFECTED IN MY VULNERABILITY.

42 I REFUSE TO BE HELD HOSTAGE BY UNFORGIVENESS.

LIE: I CAN NEVER FORGIVE MYSELF.

Therefore, there is now no condemnation
for those who are in Christ Jesus.
ROMANS 8:1

Wandering the grocery store's greeting card aisle, I noticed that the "Get Well Soon" section was unhelpful. Having just finished cancer treatment, I was sensitive to the emotional needs of those facing a long-term illness and the ways that well-meaning people often inflict pain in their efforts to alleviate it. The platitudes in many of these cards fell flat.

After much prodding from sweet friends who needed help communicating compassion to their loved ones, I created "What to Say When You Don't Know What to Say" greeting cards. The do-no-harm stationery included messages such as, "I can't imagine all you're facing, but know the rest of us live in wonder and awe of you."[1] I carried them to speaking events without expecting much, but they were gone before we could restock.

Well, not all of them. No one picked up the card pack that said "Forgive Me" on the cover. We even had people remove the "Forgive Me" cards and throw them in the trash. Now, this wasn't your typical apology card. The full card read, "Forgive me. I haven't told you as often as I should. I think about you more than you know. You are so loved and cherished."

As I stared at the pile of unsold "Forgive Me" cards collecting dust in my basement, I was reminded that forgiveness is hard. Like, *so hard*. Forgiveness is something we ask for from others, and a blessing we try to offer freely to others, but extend it to ourselves? Forget it. Forgiving ourselves is often far more difficult than forgiving our enemies.

For years, I nannied for an incredible family with four children. We built forts, tackled homework, and read books before bed. I celebrated milestones ranging from walking and talking to trying out for the football team. I grew particularly close to the oldest child. We shared the same birthday. When I moved away to pursue a relationship with Leif, I missed the family terribly. Soon I was engaged, then married, living far away in Alaska. I failed to reach out, to stay in touch.

Then I received the news that the oldest child, who I loved so much, had taken his life. My soul shattered into a thousand pieces. I lashed myself with what-if questions: What if I had been a better nanny, a better listener, a better friend? What if I had nurtured the relationship instead of becoming wrapped up in my own life? What if I could have said something that made a difference? I couldn't forgive myself for failing to communicate and demonstrate how much he was treasured, loved, and celebrated.

Maybe you drove the car that injured someone. Or you battled an addiction that took a heavy toll on your family. Or your grown son suffers from insecurities you know you caused. Or you served in the military and can't forgive yourself for the shots you fired. The scenes replay in your mind. The haunting memories chase you down and wake you up at night in a cold sweat.

> THE FORGIVENESS THAT COMES FROM JESUS IS DESIGNED TO FLOW TO YOU AND THROUGH YOU.

The Accuser wants you to make an agreement: "I can never forgive myself." That way you'll continue making emotional payments on an ever-increasing bill—until you are embroiled in self-hatred. That's how he snuffs out your potential and makes you ineffective.

Christ came to set you free from unforgiveness. He paid the penalty for your sins, your failures, your shortcomings on the cross once and for all. The forgiveness that comes from Jesus is designed to flow to you and through you. Because of his sacrifice, God forgives you and you can forgive yourself. You are not more powerful than God, and you cannot keep a debt he's already paid.

Now, the Enemy will not give up easily. I've discovered this over the years as the what-ifs continue to swirl around that child I loved so much. The Accuser loves to throw memories and feelings back at us, not because he has a case anymore, but because he wants to paralyze us with guilt and shame. We must remember that God's kingdom has a double indemnity law: you cannot be convicted of the same crime twice. We must embrace the work Jesus did on the cross and remind the Accuser the case is closed.

There's no condemnation for followers of Jesus (Romans 8:1). Refuse to do the Enemy's bidding any longer. Give yourself a "Forgive Me" card today and walk in the fullness of freedom.

DECLARATION
I REFUSE TO BE HELD HOSTAGE BY UNFORGIVENESS.

43 I WILL FORGIVE SEVEN TIMES SEVENTY AND BEYOND BECAUSE I AM FORGIVEN.

LIE: WHAT THEY DID IS UNFORGIVABLE.

Jesus said to him, "I do not say to you seven times, but seventy-seven times."

MATTHEW 18:22 ESV

A few years ago, Leif and I decided to sign a contract with a payroll company to simplify our ministry finances. Leif spent weeks researching payroll companies and found one with a Better Business Bureau A+ rating. As part of the package, the company we hired was to withhold money to pay our taxes each month.

Everything went swimmingly for the first year; then we received a notice that we'd missed a payment to the IRS. We called and the issue was fixed—or so we thought. Months later, a series of letters from the IRS landed in our mailbox. That's when an accountant informed me that while the payroll company had withdrawn the funds from our accounts, they had never paid our taxes. They had pocketed the money for almost a year. We had been embezzled.

We were on the hook for taxes, fees, and penalties equivalent to almost a year's wages. The payroll company declared bankruptcy to skirt their responsibility and then opened up shop in a different state to scam more people.

To me, the company's actions were unforgivable. I whined about the injustice to anyone and everyone who would listen—the IRS, local law enforcement, government representatives, my dog groomer. Justice never came.

In the mire of my brokenness, I knew I needed to forgive those embezzlers, but the thought made me woozy. They violated our trust. The thievery cost us wads of money, countless hours, and immeasurable stress—not to mention a heavy emotional toll. Forgiveness promised freedom, but I resisted. Soon I found myself nodding in hearty agreement with the Accuser, who whispered, "What they did is unforgivable."

Refusing to forgive left me distrustful. My ire was doled out toward anyone who broke the most innocent of promises. If you said you'd bring a salad to dinner and forgot, I felt betrayed. If you promised to meet me at the movie theater on the hour and arrived four minutes late, I felt you were out to get me. I fumed at tiny inconsistencies and lived on high alert for anyone who might be a shyster.

Then I stumbled on what felt at the time like the Bible's most annoying story. Peter asks Jesus to crunch some numbers in the arithmetic of forgiveness. He wants to know how many times he needs to forgive, suggesting up to seven times (Matthew 18:21). The number seemed generous to me. What about a three-strikes-and-you're-out policy?

Jesus says that's only a fraction of what's required. He tells Peter to stop counting and move to multiplication. We must forgive seventy times seven—more than anyone feels like offering and more than anyone wants to endure.

In Hebrew the word *seven* carries the meaning of wholeness. Jesus gives his disciples more than a number; he ushers in a new way of life. In essence, Jesus says, "Forgive wholly and you will find yourself whole; forgive completely and you will find yourself complete."

"FORGIVE WHOLLY AND YOU WILL FIND YOURSELF WHOLE."

Perhaps that's why Jesus tells Peter to forgive seventy times seven: he knows how long it takes for us humans to offer *total* forgiveness. For me, forgiveness took root somewhere between 372 and 379 times. I finally stopped counting, and forgiveness flooded the deep recesses of my heart.

Guess what? It feels good. I'm no longer eaten up by negativity and a lust for justice. What they did was wrong, and forgiving them hasn't made it right. But my soul is healthy regardless of them.

I don't know what "they" have done to you that seems unforgivable. But trust me: harboring that grudge is harming you much more than them.

DECLARATION
I WILL FORGIVE SEVEN TIMES SEVENTY AND BEYOND BECAUSE I AM FORGIVEN.

44 I AM AN OVERCOMER.

For everyone born of God overcomes the world. This is the
victory that has overcome the world, even our faith.
1 JOHN 5:4

A six-foot-eight Norwegian by the name of Leif swept me off my feet
years ago. On an early date, he asked me about my favorite book of
the Bible. I shared mine—the gospel of John—then asked about his.

"Philippians," he said without hesitation.

"Why?" I pressed.

"Because it teaches me how to love God and others—and how to overcome everyday challenges," Leif explained.

I've returned to study this power-packed letter dozens of times since
that early date with my now-hubby. Each time I'm struck by the prac-
tical wisdom within. The apostle Paul planted churches throughout
the Roman Empire. He loved each one. Yet he had a special affection

for the church at Philippi. This precious congregation tugged at an overworked, aging apostle's heartstrings.

Detained in Rome for preaching Jesus, Paul penned his words from a cramped, dingy cell. Ancient prisons were precarious places. Inmates depended on friends, family, and outsiders to provide meals and supplies. If no one appeared, the prisoners starved or froze.

By the time Paul writes this letter, he feels everyone has deserted him except Timothy. He has every reason to believe the lie "I might as well give up." Yet he clings to the hope found in Christ as an overcomer.

YOU'RE MORE THAN A CONQUEROR.

When an old friend, Epaphroditus, appears outside the cell (Philippians 2:25), Paul is flabbergasted. He soon discovers the church at Philippi hadn't known about his hardship. As soon as they learned of the apostle's situation, they pooled resources and sent Epaphroditus. This friend trekked forty days by foot to make the visit.

Epaphroditus's presence grounds Paul in the truth that he's neither alone nor forgotten. With his soul refreshed, Paul writes a thank-you letter to the church at Philippi:

I want you to know, brethren, that the things which happened to me have actually turned out for the furtherance of the gospel, so that it has become evident to the whole palace guard, and to all the rest, that my chains are in Christ. (Philippians 1:12–13 NKJV)

Notice Paul doesn't focus on the squeaky rats, looming prison guards, or cramped cell life. Rather than inform his readers of his life as a prisoner, he zeroes in on his perspective on the work of Christ. Like a football coach who interprets the dropped pass in a positive way at halftime, Paul argues that what appears to be a brutal loss is leading up to a triumphant victory.

Rather than collapse under the pressure of Rome's brutal penal system, the gospel flourishes. Paul refuses to be defeated by prison bars and in the process reveals himself as an overcomer.[1]

You'll notice Paul doesn't allow his feelings of disappointment or abandonment to overcome him. When hardship lands on your front porch, you may be tempted to withdraw or walk away. In those moments the Accuser will bellow, "Just give up!"

Yet even in the midst of your worst day, Christ is at work. In all that you face, you are more than a conqueror through Jesus, who loves you and gave up his life for you (Romans 8:37). Stand in God's power and declare that today's troubles will not rob you of future wins.

DECLARATION
I AM
AN OVERCOMER.

45 I REFUSE TO BOW MY KNEE TO THE ACCUSER.

LIE: CHRISTIANS ARE THE WORST.

He has delivered us from the power of darkness and
conveyed us into the kingdom of the Son of His love.
COLOSSIANS 1:13 NKJV

I met an elderly woman once who had weathered some storms. She
had finished serving as a missionary in China and shared with me the
hope and expectation of all that God was doing in the church over-
seas. She spoke of their faith under persecution and fervent prayer. But
when she spoke of the church in America, her face fell.

She tore into Christians who lived in the US. She spoke of believers'
materialism and concern for self-preservation. She noted our com-
placency and lack of spiritual discipline. She pointed to Christians'
loss of faith and preoccupation with worldly goods. I listened
patiently because of some truth in her words. I'd seen much of what
she'd seen.

But her venom revealed that she had come to agree with one of the Accuser's most popular lies today: "Christians are the worst." This lie has caught on with ferocity and velocity both in pop culture and among the faithful.

Those outside the church see Christians as judgmental, hypocritical, power-hungry, bigoted. Spend five minutes on social media, and you'll collect more than enough evidence to support this argument. Those inside the church tout stories of backbiting, betrayal, and belittling. And, well, who can argue that those problems aren't prevalent among Christians?

Yet God remains at work among us as "He has delivered *us* from the power of darkness and conveyed *us* into the kingdom of the Son of His love" (Colossians 1:13 NKJV, emphasis added).

Maybe you've grown tired of religious leaders who act like celebrities and the Christians who treat them that way. Or you joined a Bible study group only to feel invisible. Or maybe you're tired of having to apologize for what a Christian pastor said on a national news outlet that day. Or a sermon that sounds more like a story than an exposition of Scripture. Or another video series that transforms church into a spiritual entertainment hub. Or another gathering where food and fellowship are the main courses, and Jesus is barely on the periphery.

You may find your breaking point over the new building fund, a change in leadership, a moral failing of your leadership, the size of house your pastor lives in, or the brand of sneakers your pastor wears. And now you, too, find yourself thinking, *Christians are the worst.* The Accuser would love for you to believe this deep in your sinew. Because if he can pick you off and isolate you, he can get you to agree with him more.

Jesus gives us fair warning of what Christians can expect: "It is not the healthy who need a doctor, but the sick. I have not come to call the righteous, but sinners" (Mark 2:17).

It's easy to think of church as a day spa complete with cherub-shaped ice cubes. But it's really more like a military hospital on the front lines. Vicious attacks. Walking wounded. People struggling with PTSD. Bodies, barely clinging to life, carried in on gurneys. Chaos and carnage mingling with healing and hope. The good news is that Jesus likes to show up among the fragmented, wounded, poverty-stricken, and desperate.

THE CHURCH IS STILL THE BRIDE OF CHRIST.

I realize American churches are far from perfect, and many have gone astray, but the church is still the bride of Christ, and her members are still the sons and daughters of God. The bride may have holes in her dress, stains on her shoes, and makeup smeared on her face, but she is still the bride.

The Scriptures says that God is constructing a mysterious, invisible spiritual temple in our midst (Ephesians 2:19–22). His handiwork is displayed in the physical church, the assemblies of Christians gathered together as a tangible expression of God-life to the world. Anyone with a pulse can point out the ragamuffin qualities of a local assembly, but if you choose only to see the stains, then you'll soon lose focus on the hope of Christ's bride.

When we recognize that God's perspective on the church differs from ours, then we will begin treating her with the care she deserves. Instead of tearing her down, we will build her up and unleash her power into the world.

DECLARATION
I REFUSE TO BOW MY
KNEE TO THE ACCUSER.

46 I WILL NOT LISTEN TO THE VOICE OF THE ADVERSARY.

LIE: THEY ARE NEVER GOING TO CHANGE.

"The thief comes only to steal and kill and destroy; I have come that they may have life, and have it to the full."
JOHN 10:10

One of my favorite games to play with my five-year-old buddy, Carter, is I Spy. We'll sit in a room in church or on the front porch of his parents' home, and one of us will announce, "I spy something green." Then a series of yes-or-no questions proceed. "Is it your shirt?" "Is it that sign?" "Is it that plant?" Until—voilà—the object is identified. We celebrate and then pick a new item for another round of I Spy.

During a recent prayer time, I imagined myself sitting beside Jesus, and this game came to mind. Suddenly, I felt compelled to bring to him the names of people I knew.

I remembered Marcus, who had recently been laid off from his job in ministry. I asked Jesus, "What do you spy?"

The thought popped into my mind, *Marcus is being transitioned into a greater role in my kingdom.*

Then there was Annie, who felt overwhelmed by motherhood. *Annie is being raised up to depend on me and experience deeper levels of my affection.*

I remembered Krista and Dan, whose marriage had become rocky. *In their lives—individual and together—I'm rising with healing in my wings.*

Name after name came to mind until I asked Jesus, "What do you spy when you see me?"

A single sentence shattered the silence: "I spy someone deeply loved."

I could feel my shoulders lower and my heartbeat slow. With those words, I was reminded that I—and everyone whose name I whispered to Jesus—am ever and always held in his loving embrace. That Christ is with us and for us even when it appears he might be on a lunch break.

Jesus always breathes new life, new hope, new healing into you and me. When Christ sees you, he whispers, "I spy someone deeply loved."

Remember, the Adversary plays I Spy too. Yet his tactics never result in wholeness and restoration. The Enemy fumes accusations, destruction, death. Lies like, "I spy a person who is never going to change, a situation beyond redemption, a marriage that can never be reconciled."

WHEN CHRIST SEES YOU, HE WHISPERS, "I SPY SOMEONE DEEPLY LOVED."

He longs to woo you into his dark playground until you toy with his accusations. If left unchecked, you'll see the worst in others instead of their God-given worth. You'll focus on others' faults instead of God's faithfulness. You'll zero in on others' weaknesses instead of God's will for their lives.

The Enemy's version of I Spy highlights flaws and failings, warts and wrongdoings.

Yet you don't have to listen to the voice of the Adversary. You have the power through King Jesus, who has already won the war, to break every agreement with darkness and live as a child of light. Jesus says, "The thief comes only to steal and kill and destroy; I have come that they may have life, and have it to the full" (John 10:10). Christ comes to you with life-giving power to overcome.

You can wake up each day and declare that you will not listen to the voice of the Adversary. That you will view the world through the lens of Christ. You can play I Spy with Jesus by simply asking, "God, what do you see when you look at this person?"

The answer might surprise you and set you free.

DECLARATION
I WILL NOT LISTEN TO THE VOICE OF THE ADVERSARY.

47 I WILL NOT FLINCH IN THE FACE OF ADVERSITY

LIE: THAT WON'T HAPPEN TO ME.

Dear friends, do not be surprised at the fiery ordeal that has come on you to test you, as though something strange were happening to you.
1 PETER 4:12

In my life and ministry, I've experienced rejection, false accusations, embezzlement, belittlement, and betrayal. I've battled mysterious illnesses and aggressive cancer. With each hardship, my illusion that those kinds of things happen only to other people has been dismantled.

First Peter says we shouldn't be surprised when adversity enters our lives. In fact, expect it. Jesus refutes the magical thinking that bad things won't happen to us if we follow certain formulas. He reminds us that God causes the sun to rise on the evil and the good and sends rain on the righteous and the unrighteous (Matthew 5:45). In this passage, Jesus addresses more than dawn, dusk, and weather patterns. He teaches that good things happen to all people. And terrible things do too.

Hardship and adversity are unavoidable parts every life, but as God's children, we do not face them alone. The apostle Paul describes our remarkable resilience: "We are hard pressed on every side, but not crushed; perplexed, but not in despair; persecuted, but not abandoned; struck down, but not destroyed" (2 Corinthians 4:8–9).

THE HARDSHIPS WE FACE IN LIFE MAY *REFINE* US, BUT THEY DO NOT HAVE TO *DEFINE* US.

The power of a resurrected Christ rests outside your crushing circumstances and heartbreaking hardships. This power, which is yours through the Holy Spirit, can change you. It can enable you to do far more than you ever could in your own strength.

Through the power of Christ, your circumstances can no longer hold you captive. Yes, you are more than an overcomer.

Paul isn't asking whether bad things happen to people who follow Jesus. He knows they happen. Yet this knowledge doesn't seem to steal an ounce of his trust in God. He knows the hardships we face in life may *refine* us, but they do not have to *define* us. In every situation, we can turn toward the One who saves us from being crushed and abandoned.

I'm sorry to inform you that becoming a follower of Jesus fails to inoculate you from hardship. But when difficulty shows up unannounced, it does not possess the power to destroy you. Thanks to the Holy Spirit, you do not have to be surprised or flinch in the face of adversity.

DECLARATION
I WILL NOT FLINCH IN THE FACE OF ADVERSITY.

48 GOD WORKS ALL THINGS TOGETHER.

LIE: EVERYTHING BAD HAPPENS TO ME.

And we know that in all things God works for the good of those who love him, who have been called according to his purpose.
ROMANS 8:28

Sometimes life knocks you flat on the floor. That happened literally to me a few years ago.

Leif and I were living in Denver at the time, and we had been capsized by a wave of unforeseen difficulties. First, our only car's transmission blew out when we were two hours from our home—and at least as far from the nearest repair shop. We were carless for two weeks, waiting for the repair shop to finish the work.

Then the day before I picked up the vehicle, I walked downstairs to place fresh linens on our guest bed and noticed my socks felt moist. An old copper water pipe had ruptured, flooding our basement.

Around the same time, several of our clients informed us they were unable to pay us what they owed. Though we might have been able to absorb the loss at a different time, our financial margin was eroded by the unexpected car and flood repairs.

Next, a friendship I'd been trying to mend became irreparable, and I mourned the loss.

And that's when it happened. Blap! Falling to the kitchen floor, I gave in to the weeping. This wasn't my first encounter with difficulty, and I knew it wouldn't be my last, but this experience felt different due to the compounding effect. It's what a military general might call "shock and awe," a spectacular display of force that paralyzes an adversary's perception of the battle, destroying its will to fight.

Crumbs, like sand, ground against my limbs. A holy stanza emerged from the recesses of my soul as I lay flat on the floor pressed against the hardwood:

God is good.
God is on the throne.
Breathe in.
Breathe out.

I repeated the refrain over and over, in between gasps and heaves. I wasn't only speaking to God; God was speaking to me too. For months, I had been so focused on the pain, the problems, the perplexities, that I was missing out on the presence of God.

Hope arrived in declaring Psalm 27:13: "I would have despaired unless I had believed that I would see the goodness of the LORD in the land of the living" (NASB). I recited this powerful passage dozens of times that day and every day for weeks afterward. This scripture grounded me in the truth that God was still working all things together even as life fell apart.

Sooner or later, we all encounter a situation that steals our strength and smacks us down. The moment leaves us with unanswerable questions. *Why this? Why now? Why again?* When we ask such questions to the exclusion of all else, the Accuser

GOD NEVER STUMBLES.

whispers, "God isn't paying attention to you and what you're facing. He's far away and has left you to your own devices." In desperation, we're tempted to abandon our trust in God and make this destructive agreement.

Instead, we must breathe deeply and declare that God's goodness remains and that King Jesus is still on the throne. Just because God *feels* far away doesn't mean God *is* far away. Just because life is falling apart does not mean God is not still holding all things together. On the kitchen floor, I rediscovered that even when I lose my footing, God never stumbles. Not a single tear slips by his sight. Not a single groan escapes his ear.

When life catches you off guard, God remains good. He is still working all things together. When you feel God has disappeared and left you for dead, remember that he is still near. When you're taken off guard, remind yourself that he is right with you and is not surprised. Keep breathing and keep trusting that God will meet you wherever you may find yourself.

DECLARATION
GOD WORKS
ALL THINGS TOGETHER.

49 GOD WORKS FOR MY GOOD.

LIE: EVERYTHING IS AGAINST ME.

Rise up and help us; rescue us because of your unfailing love.
PSALM 44:26

The day began like any other. I nestled on the couch for some spiritual reflection. I could hear birds chirping outside the window just beyond our back deck. Our super-pup, Zoom, nestled on the back of the couch near my shoulder. All was calm and quiet, and then—blurp!—Zoom stood up and vomited all over my shoulder and arm.

I set my queasy pooch outside for a few minutes, took a quick shower, and switched into a fresh set of clothes. That's when I slipped and bonked my head on the bathroom wall. The throbbing pain put me on edge, so I grabbed some ice from the freezer. And then I saw the kitchen clock and realized I was twenty minutes late for an important conference call. By the time I jumped on, the other participants had left. I'd missed it completely, and it took weeks to reschedule.

But the day wasn't done unraveling.

While I worked on a document, the computer froze. AutoSave failed, and my work was lost. The person I was scheduled to meet for lunch no-showed. One of our employees became sick, and we missed a crucial deadline. Leif's day was a swirl of stress, too, so at supper we ate leftovers across from each other in exhausted silence.

Toward the end of the evening, I cuddled up with Zoom to rest. I gazed deep into my pup's eyes with gratitude for his undying love for me. And then—blurp!—he threw up on me again. *Seriously, God?*

Have you ever had a day when you felt like everything was against you, and you couldn't make it stop? We all have terrible, awful, no good, very bad days when it's hard to believe the promise that God works for the good of those who love him. It's even harder in those longer seasons of life, like a pandemic, when we're battling depression or disease, addiction or betrayal.

Either way—a single bad day or a series of horrible ones that seems to have no end—the apostle Paul reminds us in Romans 8:28 that God is with us and a step ahead of us, working on our behalf. Sometimes he's behind the scenes, completely unseen, but he's always working to bring about his good purposes for his people.

If you're facing a hard time, today's declaration might sound cliché or like an empty promise. Yet God is willing and able to redeem every situation and circumstance. Notice that Paul doesn't say everything is good. Cancer is not good. Abuse is not good. Covid-19 is not good. Racism is not good.

GOD IS WILLING AND ABLE TO REDEEM EVERY SITUATION.

As followers of God, we must do all we can to eliminate these from the world. But what we face *can* be redeemed by God for good. How do we know? Because this is demonstrated time and time again in the life of Christ.

In the gospel of Mark, we read of women who go to the tomb of Jesus on a dismal Sunday morning. These women and the disciples have seen their Savior withstand an unfair trial and receive the death penalty. Mary has watched her son brutally murdered. The people of God have waited for a new king, but the Roman Empire still rules and reigns. Each of these people feels the weight of hopelessness.

Then, as the women arrive to anoint Jesus' corpse, they see that the stone has been rolled away. The body, gone. They probably think it's been stolen by grave robbers or Roman leaders. Mark 16:8 describes, "Trembling and bewildered, the women went out and fled from the tomb. They said nothing to anyone, because they were afraid."

Often, we feel bewildered when God doesn't behave as we expect. When you don't get the promotion or get pregnant or find true love, it's easy to begin blaming God. Maybe you've become angry and exasperated that God hasn't come through in the way you've been hoping or anticipating. Perhaps you've forgotten that even when everything is bad, God is still working for your good and his glory.

In these moments, you need to tell the Accuser to shove it. Everything is not against you, and nothing in your life is beyond God's redemption. In God's hands, the darkness of the tomb can become a portal to new life. It's in the midst of your *Seriously, God?* moments that God can seriously work miracles.

DECLARATION
GOD WORKS
FOR MY GOOD.

50 GOD WORKS FOR HIS GLORY.

"I know the plans I have for you," declares the LORD, "plans to prosper you and not to harm you, plans to give you hope and a future."
JEREMIAH 29:11

Several years ago, I traveled to spend time with a shepherd, a bee-keeper, a farmer, and a vintner in order to understand the Bible's rich agricultural imagery. The Scripture came alive on my journeys. Yet one of the greatest spiritual lessons from that time came not so much from these fascinating people but from watching some geese wander around a barn. They kept walking in circles. One day I finally asked my host, "What are they looking for?"

"They're looking for their eggs," she said.

"Where are they?" I asked.

"I threw them in the creek."

My eyes bugged in disbelief. I couldn't help blurting out, "Why!?" Her actions seemed cold and cruel, a far cry from the typical caring ways of this woman who loved all her animals.

"Because they were infertile," my host said. "They would never hatch. I needed to get these geese back to their regular life. They've been sitting on infertile eggs for three months. The only way to get them back to the life they're supposed to be living is to take away their dead eggs."

Her answer helped me see her action as one of compassion and wisdom. I couldn't help but wonder how often I have sat on dreams that were never going to hatch, or worse, sat on the empty promises of the Enemy that would never yield life.

One of the greatest lies we can believe is that we're stuck, that there's no way forward, there's no hope, there's no future, unless this one teeny tiny thing comes to pass in exactly the way we desire and at the moment we expect with the help of all the people we've convinced ourselves are necessary. When it doesn't come to pass, we make an agreement with the Accuser that there's no way out.

GOD HAS A HOPE AND A FUTURE FOR US.

Throughout Scripture, we are reminded that God has a hope and a future for us. As the prophet Jeremiah reminded the people of Israel, "'For I know the plans I have for you,' declares the LORD, 'plans to prosper you and not to harm you, plans to give you hope and a future'" (Jeremiah 29:11).

Often, when it appears there's no way out, God displays his power. When the Israelites find themselves pinned against the Red Sea, God splits the water and allows them to cross on dry ground. When the Philistines hem in the Israelites, God slays a giant and brings victory through a stone-slinging shepherd. When three young men are tossed into an inferno, the flames of adversity don't singe them. When all of humanity is trapped by darkness, sin, and shame, God sends Jesus to illuminate, liberate, and form us into Christ's likeness.

Like those geese, you may be sitting on broken dreams, disappointments, and losses. You may think there's no way out. You may have even begun to doubt God's presence. But that couldn't be further from the truth. It's time to get up and get moving. Even in this, God is working all things together for your good and his glory—that you may become more Christlike.

God invites you to release your concerns to him so you can get back to the life you were created for.

DECLARATION
GOD WORKS
FOR HIS GLORY.

51 I WILL LOOK FOR THE CHARACTER AND COMPETENCE OF GOD IN EVERY SITUATION.

LIE: THIS WON'T END WELL.

Now to him who is able to do immeasurably more than all we ask or imagine . . .
EPHESIANS 3:20

What do you do when you're caught between an immovable rock and an impossible place? An unpronounceable diagnosis. A prodigal child. Unemployment. Impending financial collapse. The stress of caring for aging parents as well as your children. It's tempting to believe that a terrible ending to the harrowing story is not only probable but inevitable.

"This won't end well," the Accuser says. His words seem to align with the facts and what you feel in your gut. You make an agreement and begin reordering your life as if the awful future you fear has already arrived.

If you read the New Testament epistles, you will notice that the apostle Paul is no Pollyanna. He never offers pie-in-the-sky thinking or baseless optimism. Which is why his declarations when trapped behind bars with an uncertain future are so powerful. Paul proclaims that what has happened will turn out for his deliverance (Philippians 1:19).

Paul's words are not his own; he's riffing on the ancient book of Job. Those are the exact words Job speaks after he loses his children and his home, his wealth and his health. The sudden, brutal losses leave Job scraping his wounds with pottery shards, despairing about the future.

Job's friends surround him. For the first seven days, they sit in silence and mourn with Job. Their presence brings consolation. On the eighth day, they open their mouths and the whole scene spirals. Rather than speak words that assuage his pain, they align their thoughts and words with the Accuser. They tell Job that his wounds are self-inflicted from a hidden sin in his life. In the process, they pour acid on his unexplainable pain.

Job believes that he'll be vindicated in the end. Rather than tumble into despair, Job clings to the promise of rescue: "Indeed, this will turn out for my deliverance" (Job 13:16).

Centuries later, Paul proclaims the same promise. Notice Paul doesn't place his faith in a particular outcome. He doesn't claim that he will be delivered from prison or even death. Instead, he stands on two steady pillars: God's character and God's competence.

The Bible teaches that God is more dependable than gravity. He never changes (Malachi 3:6). His purposes are unfailing, his promises trustworthy, his presence guaranteed. God is also self-sufficient. That means he possesses the unlimited resources of grace, goodness, power, and strength. No matter what you need, God will never run out (Philippians 4:19). Nothing is too difficult for him (Jeremiah 32:27).

GOD IS MORE DEPENDABLE THAN GRAVITY.

It's easy to stand on God's faithfulness and power when I reflect on his character, but I often second-guess his competency. That's why I insert myself into situations where I don't belong. I open my mouth when I should bite my tongue. Snatch the steering wheel when I should ride shotgun.

Each day I must commit, "I will look for the character and competence of God in every situation."[1] This declaration forces me to search for God in life's finest details. To note the competency of God in situations where I hadn't considered his presence—including those where I told myself, "This won't end well."

Even in dicey situations, Job and Paul hold fast to God as their fortress and rock, refuge and shield, salvation, and stronghold (Psalm 18:2). Trusting in God's character and competence gives them and us the courage to proclaim with boldness, "This will turn out for my deliverance." Declare this truth in your life and watch God transform your pessimism into positivity.

DECLARATION
I WILL LOOK FOR THE CHARACTER AND COMPETENCE OF GOD IN EVERY SITUATION.

52 I AM ON GOD'S OFFENSIVE TEAM TODAY.

He saw heaven being torn open and the Spirit descending on him like a dove.

MARK 1:10

When the curtain peels back on Mark's gospel, we're greeted with a strange fellow named John the Baptizer in a camel-fur coat. We are told he has come to proclaim the impending arrival of the Chosen One, the Messiah. Without skipping a beat, Jesus himself enters the act and John baptizes him.

> Just as Jesus was coming up out of the water, he saw heaven being torn open and the Spirit descending on him like a dove. (Mark 1:10)

The Greek word Mark uses here, *schizó*, means to tear open. This same word is used again in Mark's gospel—at Christ's death. Mark describes the veil between heaven and earth being ripped open. This symbol reminds the Jewish audience of the curtain inside the temple that kept man from God.

Matthew and Luke appear more restrained than Mark. They tame their language when they retell Jesus' baptism. Rather than use the word meaning "to tear open," they employ a more passive approach, using "was opened" (Matthew 3:16; Luke 3:21).

Mark uses the violent, jolting word to emphasize an important truth: at Christ's baptism and at Christ's death, heaven comes to earth. Through Christ, God tears through all that stands between us and him. God doesn't passively wait for an invitation into earth, standing on the doorstep to be let in. God is ripping open the heavens and tearing down the walls to unleash his kingdom and power on earth. The best part? It's still happening.

THROUGH CHRIST, GOD TEARS THROUGH ALL THAT STANDS BETWEEN US AND HIM.

The kingdom of God advances among dinner tables and church pews, in doctor's offices and cubicles, in the carpool pick-up line, and *maaaaaaybe* even while you're on hold with the customer service agent. The kingdom of God tears in whenever you allow Christ's love to saturate you and spill out onto those around you.

If you have come to believe the Accuser's lie that what you do does not matter, break that agreement immediately. Do not believe for one hot minute that what you do has no impact. The Enemy doesn't want you to play on the offensive team of God's kingdom. He wants to sideline you.

You are a kingdom bearer. You are anointed to declare good news to the poor, bind up the brokenhearted, proclaim freedom to the captives, and release prisoners from the darkness. You are on God's offensive team today, and—spoiler alert—we win!

DECLARATION
I AM ON
GOD'S OFFENSIVE TEAM TODAY.

THE 90-SECOND DAILY CHALLENGE: POWERFUL DAILY DECLARATIONS WITH SCRIPTURE REFERENCES

- ❋ Jesus is King of my life (Exodus 20:3; Psalm 29:10–11; Acts 2:33–36; Revelation 5:11–14).
- ❋ I am who Christ says I am (Ephesians 1:13–14; Colossians 3:3, 12; 1 Peter 2:9).
- ❋ I take every thought captive (Lamentations 3:20–24; Romans 12:2; 2 Corinthians 10:5; Philippians 4:8–9).
- ❋ I break every agreement that sets itself up against the knowledge of God (Isaiah 28:15–18, 29; 2 Corinthians 6:16; 10:5; Hebrews 12:1–3; 1 John 5:6–12, 20).
- ❋ My purpose is to love, serve, glorify, and enjoy God forever (Deuteronomy 6:4–5; Joshua 22:5; Psalm 37:4; 100:1–5; Isaiah 61:10; Matthew 22:35–40; Mark 12:28–31; Luke 10:25–28; Acts 17:28; Romans 3:23–24; 1 Corinthians 8:6; 10:31; 1 John 4:19).
- ❋ I am filled with the Holy Spirit (John 14:26; 1 Corinthians 6:19; 2 Corinthians 1:21–22; 3:17–18; Galatians 5:25; Ephesians 1:13–14; Titus 3:4–7).
- ❋ The same power that resurrected Christ from the dead lives in me (Romans 8:11; Ephesians 1:15–23, especially 19–20; Hebrews 13:20–21).

- I am God's beloved child, in whom he is well pleased (Genesis 1:26–31; Psalm 149:4; Zephaniah 3:17; Matthew 3:17; John 1:12–13; 14:18; Ephesians 5:1–2; Colossians 3:12; 1 Thessalonians 1:4; James 1:17–18; 1 John 3:1–3).
- I am fearfully and wonderfully made (Genesis 1:26–27; 2:7, 22; Psalm 139:14), beautiful beyond measure (Deuteronomy 7:6; Ecclesiastes 3:11; Song of Songs 4:7; Isaiah 61:1–3; Zechariah 9:16–17; 2 Corinthians 3:18).
- The power of God guards my thoughts (Proverbs 2:1–5; 4:20–23; 9:10; Philippians 4:7–8), the Word of God guides my steps (Psalm 119:105; Proverbs 30:5; 1 Thessalonians 2:13; 2 Timothy 3:14–17; Hebrews 4:12), and the favor of God rests on me (Luke 2:14; 2 Corinthians 6:2; Philippians 1:2).
- Worry is not my boss (Psalm 27:1; 42:11; 86:5–7; Isaiah 41:10; Matthew 6:25; Philippians 4:6–7).
- I trust in the Lord with all my heart and lean not on my own understanding. In all my ways I will acknowledge him, and he will make my paths straight (Psalm 20:7; 28:7; 91:2; Proverbs 3:5–6; Jeremiah 39:18; Nahum 1:7; Romans 15:13).
- The Lord is my shepherd. I lack nothing. He makes me lie down in green pastures. He leads me beside still waters. He restores my soul (Psalm 23:1–3; John 10:11, 14–16; Revelation 7:9–17).
- God is my strength (Nehemiah 8:10; Psalm 28:7; 73:26; Isaiah 40:28–31; Philippians 4:13), my shield (Psalm 3:3; Proverbs 30:5; Ephesians 6:16). He's always with me (Matthew 28:20; Luke 15:31), always for me (Psalm 56:9; Romans 5:8; 8:31–34), always sees me (Genesis 16:13–14; 1 Samuel 16:7; 2 Chronicles 16:9; Psalm 33:12–15; Luke 1:46–49).

* No weapon formed against me will prosper (Psalm 91:1–16; Isaiah 2:4; 54:17; Romans 8:35–39; 1 Corinthians 15:50–58; 2 Corinthians 1:21; Ephesians 6:10–18; 2 Timothy 4:18).

* I am anointed, empowered, and called to reach people far from God (Matthew 28:18–20; Luke 4:18; John 14:12–17; Acts 1:8; Romans 1:16; Ephesians 4:7–13; 2 Peter 1:3).

* My words have power (Proverbs 18:21; Acts 15:30–34; 1 Thessalonians 5:9–11; Hebrews 3:13; James 5:13–16).

* I will look for every opportunity to speak life (Proverbs 15:4; 1 Thessalonians 5:16–18), show compassion (Matthew 14:14; Philippians 2:1–2; Colossians 3:12), and bring out the best in others (Jeremiah 29:7; 1 Corinthians 10:24; Philippians 1:9–10; Colossians 4:6; 1 Thessalonians 5:15).

* Shame is not my master (Isaiah 61:7; Romans 1:16; 5:5; 9:3–4; 10:11; 2 Timothy 1:12; Hebrews 4:16; 1 Peter 2:6; 1 John 3:20).

* God's power is perfected in my vulnerability (Romans 8:26; 1 Corinthians 1:26–31; 2 Corinthians 12:9–10; 13:4).

* I refuse to be held hostage by unforgiveness (Acts 10:43; Romans 8:1; Ephesians 4:32; Colossians 1:13–14). I will forgive seventy times seven and beyond because I am forgiven (Matthew 18:21–22; 6:12; Mark 11:25; Colossians 3:13).

* I am an overcomer (Psalm 30:1–12; 44:1–8; Romans 8:35–39; 1 Corinthians 15:54–57; 1 John 2:12–14; 5:4).

* I refuse to bow my knee to the Accuser, listen to the voice of the Adversary (John 10:10; Colossians 1:13; 1 Peter 5:8–10), or flinch in the face of adversity (Exodus 14:13; 2 Chronicles 20:17; Psalm 20:7–8; Luke 21:17; 1 Corinthians 15:58; 16:13; Philippians 1:27; 2 Thessalonians 2:15; James 5:8; 1 Peter 4:12).

※ God works all things together for my good and his glory
(Psalm 27:13; 44:26; 79:9; Isaiah 58:8; Jeremiah 29:11; John
1:14; 17:24; Romans 5:2; 8:28; 2 Corinthians 4:6, 15; 1 Peter 5:10;
Revelation 21:1–5).

※ I will look for the character and competence of God in every
situation (Daniel 3:17–18; Luke 1:37; Ephesians 3:20; 1 Timothy
6:13–16; 2 Timothy 1:8–12; Hebrews 7:25).

※ I am on God's offensive team today (Romans 14:8; Galatians
6:10; Ephesians 1:13–14; 6:7; Philippians 1:21–22; 3:13–14;
2 Timothy 4:7).

ACKNOWLEDGMENTS

Thank you to the incredible editorial and publishing team—Laura, Danielle, and Kristen. Thank you to Jonathan Merritt for being a writing iron-sharpener, pushing me to be refine and rework. I'm grateful for Tracee Hackel, Andrea Townsend, and Heidi White for their amazing editing and feedback. Thank you to Craig Groeshel for introducing me to the power of biblical declarations. Thank you to Chris and Christy Ferebee, and Carolyn and Alex Garza. Leif Oines, the love of my life, I'm so grateful you've shown me such compassion and grace. Thank you to every reader who has made this journey with me.

ABOUT THE AUTHOR

Margaret Feinberg, host of the popular *The Joycast* podcast, is one of America's most beloved Bible teachers. She speaks at churches and leading conferences including Thrive and Women of Joy. Her books, including *Fight Back with Joy*, *Scouting the Divine*, and *Taste and See*, along with their corresponding Bible studies, have sold more than one million copies and received critical acclaim as well as national media coverage from CNN, Associated Press, *USA Today*, *Los Angeles Times*, *Washington Post*, and more. *Christianity Today* named her as one of the top fifty women who are most shaping culture and the church. Margaret savors life with her husband, Leif, a pastor in Park City, Utah.

Connect with Margaret at her website: margaretfeinberg.com or on social media.

Instagram: @mafeinberg
Twitter: @mafeinberg
Facebook: Margaret Feinberg
Email: hello@margaretfeinberg.com

NOTES

The Power of Daily Declarations

1. Craig Groeschel, "The Power of Personal Declarations," *Open Network* (Life.Church blog), https://openblog.life.church/the-power-of -personal-declarations/. It's worth noting that this is not self-help psychology. It's biblical theology. We are called to repent and believe . . . to change our minds so that new ways of Christ-thinking and Christ-speaking flow through us.

Chapter 1: Jesus is King of my life.

1. Barbara Brown Taylor, *Gospel Medicine* (Boston: Cowley Publications, 1995), 126.

Chapter 3: I take every thought captive.

1. Margarita Tartakovsky, "Why Ruminating Is Unhealthy and How to Stop," PsychCentral, July 8, 2018, https://psychcentral.com/blog/why -ruminating-is-unhealthy-and-how-to-stop/.
2. D. O. Hebb, *The Organization of Behavior* (New York: Wiley & Sons, 1949), in S. Löwel and W. Singer, "Selection of Intrinsic Horizontal Connections in the Visual Cortex by Correlated Neuronal Activity," *Science*, 255 (January 10, 1992), 209–12, https://science.sciencemag. org/content/255/5041/209.long. Note that the precise sentence used is "Neurons wire together if they fire together."

Chapter 4: I break every agreement that sets itself up against the knowledge of God.

1. Curt Thompson speaks of this in one of my all-time favorite books, *The Soul of Shame: Retelling the Stories We Believe About Ourselves* (Downers Grove, IL: InterVarsity Press, 2015), 48–49.

Chapter 6: My purpose is to serve God.

1. Amy Morin, "10 Signs You're a People-Pleaser," *Psychology Today*, August 23, 2017, https://www.psychologytoday.com/us/blog/what -mentally-strong-people-dont-do/201708/10-signs-youre-people-pleaser.

Chapter 16: The favor of God rests on me.

1. Troy Champ, "Amazing Grace and Peace," sermon from January 16 and 17, 2016.

Chapter 17: Worry is not my boss.

1. Sarah G. Miller, "1 in 6 Americans Takes a Psychiatric Drug," *Scientific American*, December 23, 2016, https://www.scientificamerican .com/article/1-in-6-americans-takes-a-psychiatric-drug/.
2. Dictionary.com, s.v. "worry," accessed February 26, 2020, https://www .dictionary.com/browse/worry.
3. Morgan Kelly, "Poor Concentration: Poverty Reduces Brainpower Needed for Navigating Other Areas of Life," Princeton University, August 29, 2013, https://www.princeton.edu/news/2013/08/29/poor -concentration-poverty-reduces-brainpower-needed-navigating-other -areas-life.

Chapter 22: The Lord is my Shepherd.

1. You can read more about the lessons from the shepherdess in my book and six-session DVD Bible study, *Scouting the Divine: My Search for God in Wine, Wool, and Wild Honey* (Grand Rapids: Zondervan, 2009).

Chapter 27: God is my strength.

1. Abigail Abrams, "Yes, Impostor Syndrome Is Real. Here's How to Deal with It," *Time*, June 20, 2018, https://time.com/5312483/how-to-deal-with-impostor-syndrome/.

Chapter 30: God is always for me.

1. A. Pawlowski, "How to Worry Better," NBCNews.com, December 13, 2017, https://www.nbcnews.com/better/pop-culture/praise-worry-why-fretting-can-be-good-you-ncna757016.

Chapter 32: No weapon formed against me will prosper.

1. Nancy Colier, "Are You Ready to Stop Feeling Like a Victim?" *Psychology Today*, January 12, 2018, https://www.psychologytoday.com/us/blog/inviting-monkey-tea/201801/are-you-ready-stop-feeling-victim.

Chapter 33: I am anointed.

1. You can read more about the incredible journey and the rich meaning of olives and their oil throughout the Bible in *Taste and See: Discovering God Among Butchers, Bakers, and Fresh Food Makers* (Grand Rapids: Zondervan, 2018).

Chapter 38: I will show compassion.

1. Diana Butler Bass, *Grateful: The Transformative Power of Giving Thanks* (San Francisco: HarperOne, 2018), 66.

Chapter 41: God's power is perfected in my vulnerability.

1. Eugene Peterson, *Christ Plays in Ten Thousand Places: A Conversation in Spiritual Theology* (Grand Rapids: Eerdmans, 2005), 212.
2. Brené Brown, *Daring Greatly: How the Courage to Be Vulnerable Transforms the Way We Live, Love, Parent, and Lead* (Garden City, NY: Avery, 2013), 33.

Chapter 42: I refuse to be held hostage by unforgiveness.

1. You find some of these life-giving cards at www.margaretfeinbergstore
.com.

Chapter 44: I am an overcomer.

1. Thanks to Troy Champ and his sermon "Sharing Someone's
Suffering," June 25–26, 2016, for many of the insights into this
teaching.

Chapter 51: I will look for the character and competence of God in
every situation.

1. Dallas Willard, *The Divine Conspiracy* (New York: HarperCollins,
1998), 350.

FREE GIFTS

I am so proud of you for going on the offensive to take every thought captive, to break every agreement that rises up against the knowledge of God. In appreciation and celebration, I've put together some free gifts for you:

- Framable *More Power to You* Daily Declarations to keep nearby
- Audio of the Daily Declarations (read by Margaret) to help you memorize
- Video of Margaret speaking the Daily Declarations over you
- Custom *More Power to You* coloring pages

To receive these free gifts, simply visit morepowertoyoubook.com or email us at hello@margaretfeinberg.com.

God is a foodie who wants to transform your supper into sacrament. Margaret Feinberg invites you on a global adventure to descend into a salt mine, knead bread, harvest olives, and pluck fresh figs. What you discover will forever change the way you read the Bible—and approach every meal. Plus, you'll find delicious recipes inside.

Available now at your favorite bookstore

margaretfeinberg.com

Savor Life. Nourish Friendships. Embark on New Adventures.
www.margaretfeinberg.com

On the site you'll find:

- Giveaways
- Free e-newsletter sign-up
- Margaret's personal blog
- Interactive discussion board

- Video and audio clips
- Secret sales and promotions
- Travel schedule
- Great prices on Bible studies

become a fan on facebook
facebook.com/margaretfeinberg

become a twitter
follower
@mafeinberg

become an instagram
follower
@mafeinberg

GHTS.   I LACK NOTHING.   THE LORD IS MY SHE

H ME.   JESUS IS KING OF MY LIFE.   I AM WHO G

POSE IS TO LOVE GOD.   MY PURPOSE IS TO SERVE GOD.

HE HOLY SPIRIT.   THE SAME POWER THAT RESURRECTED

EASED.   I AM FEARFULLY AND WONDERFULLY MADE.

THOUGHTS.   I LACK NOTHING.   THE LORD IS M

D RESTS ON ME.   I TRUST IN THE LORD WITH ALL MY H

.   HE WILL MAKE MY PATHS STRAIGHT.   I LACK N

BEYOND MEASURE.   THE POWER OF GOD GUARDS MY

ON GOD'S OFFENSIVE TEAM TODAY.   GOD IS ALWAYS

RIFY GOD.   I TAKE EVERY THOGUHT CAPTIVE.   MY

PURPOSE IS TO ENJOY GOD FOREVER.   I AM FILLED WI

SS.   I AM GOD'S BELOVED CHILD IN WHOM HE IS WEL

TIFUL BEYOND MEASURE.   THE POWER OF GOD GUARD

THE WORD OF GOD GUIDES MY STEPS.   THE FAVOR O

LEDGE HIM.   I WILL NOT LEAN ON MY OWN UNDERSTAN